Jiggs Kalra's
Classic Cooking of
Rajasthan

Also by Jiggs Kalra

PRASHAD : Cooking with Indian Master
DAAWAT : An Invitation to Indian Cooking
KAMA BHOG : Foods of Love
CLASSIC COOKING OF PUNJAB
CLASSIC COOKING OF AVADH
100 BEST OF JIGGS KALRA : Zaika ka Safar

Jiggs Kalra's
Classic Cooking of
Rajasthan

with a special section on
Cuisine of Kotah
by
Maharao Brijraj Singh and Maharani Uttara Devi

Co-editors **Pushpesh Pant, Zorawar Kalra**
and **Raminder Malhotra**
Photographs by **Ian Pereira**

ALLIED PUBLISHERS PRIVATE LIMITED
NEW DELHI BANGALORE HYDERABAD AHMEDABAD
NAGPUR MUMBAI LUCKNOW CHENNAI KOLKATA

ALLIED PUBLISHERS PRIVATE LIMITED

1/13-14 Asaf Ali Road, **New Delhi**–110002
Ph.: 011-23239001 • E-mail: delhi.books@alliedpublishers.com

47/9 Prag Narain Road, Near Kalyan Bhawan, **Lucknow**–226001
Ph.: 0522-2209942 • E-mail: lko.books@alliedpublishers.com

17 Chittaranjan Avenue, **Kolkata**–700072
Ph.: 033-22129618 • E-mail: cal.books@alliedpublishers.com

15 J.N. Heredia Marg, Ballard Estate, **Mumbai**–400001
Ph.: 022-42126969 • E-mail: mumbai.books@alliedpublishers.com

60 Shiv Sunder Apartments (Ground Floor), Central Bazar Road,
Bajaj Nagar, **Nagpur**–440010
Ph.: 0712-2234210 • E-mail: ngp.books@alliedpublishers.com

F-1 Sun House (First Floor), C.G. Road, Navrangpura,
Ellisbridge P.O., **Ahmedabad**–380006
Ph.: 079-26465916 • E-mail: ahmbd.books@alliedpublishers.com

751 Anna Salai, **Chennai**–600002
Ph.: 044-28523938 • E-mail: chennai.books@alliedpublishers.com

5th Main Road, Gandhinagar, **Bangalore**–560009
Ph.: 080-22262081 • E-mail: bngl.books@alliedpublishers.com

3-2-844/6 & 7 Kachiguda Station Road, **Hyderabad**–500027
Ph.: 040-24619079 • E-mail: hyd.books@alliedpublishers.com

Website: www.alliedpublishers.com

New edition, 2013
First published, 2005
Reprinted 2006

© Photographs : Ian Pereira and Maharao Brijraj Singh

© Jiggs Kalra & Maharao Brijraj Singh and Maharani Uttara Devi

ISBN : 978-81-8424-838-8

Published by Sunil Sachdev and printed by Ravi Sachdev at Allied Publishers Private Limited,
Printing Division, A-104 Mayapuri Phase II, New Delhi - 110064

*Dedicated
to
Late Rani Meena Ranawat of Bambulia, Kotah*
1st Dec 1957 to 27th July 2008
w/o M. Abhimanyu Singh of Bambulia, Kotah
whose original recipes are incorporated in this book.

The Bambulia family are descendants of the fifth ruler of Kotah, Rao Kishore Singh of Kotah(r.1684-96 A.D.). Maharao Durjansal of Kotah (r.1723-56) granted M.Soorajmal the jagir of Atun or Atoon/Bambulia.

Acknowledgements

I am indebted to M. Abhimanyu Singh and his gracious wife, late Rani Meena Ranawat of Bambulia, Kotah whose recipes are incorporated in this book.

I must also acknowledge the help of Shri Gyan Chand Jain for the section on the cuisine of the Merchant Princes.

My guardian angel, Jayshree Kurup, who has been nursing me since I suffered a stroke some years ago, deserves a special word of thanks for all her help in putting this work together.

I thank my Publishers, Sunil and Ravi Sachdev, and my wife, Lovejeet and sons Zorawar and Ajit for their constant encouragement in all my endeavours.

–Jiggs Kalra

Introduction

Jiggs Kalra & Pushpesh Pant

Rajasthan or the 'Land of Kings' is also known as the Cradle of Chivalry. The scorching sands of Thar, the great desert, that stretches out for miles, have for centuries witnessed unmatched scenes of valour. This is where historic battles have been fought to defend one's home and hearth and above all to preserve honour. Memories are yet green of fabulous beauties like the Princess Padmini of Chittor and legendary warriors like Rana Sanga. The traditional song of welcome refers to *Rang Rangilo Rajasthani* that translates as 'the tract of land resplendent with many hues'. This is indeed an apt description of a magical realm. The landscape is dotted with impregnable forts like Mehrangarh, cities enclosed in citadels like Chittor, beautiful palaces like the Lake Palace at Udaipur sparkling like precious gems set in precious ornaments. The bright splash of turbans and *ghagra cholis* in tie-and-dye or draperies decorated with mirror-work cast a bewitching spell on the visitors. The food in Rajasthan is no less alluring than its rainbow-hued costumes, seductive beauty of the landscape and delicate miniature paintings.

Jaipur, the Pink City, is one of the most beautiful in the land. It was built during the reign of Sawai Jaisingh II in the last quarter of the 17th century. Planned by the gifted Bengali architect Vidyadhar, it has wide roads and streets, palaces, elegant buildings and impressive market plazas, an observatory and many places of worship for Hindus and Muslims. The city nestles under the shadow of guarding forts Nahargarh and Jaigarh perched atop the hillocks encircling it and lies a short distance away from the old capital of the Kachwaha rulers at Amer. Jaipur is famous for its diamond cutters, bespoke marble statues, light as feather, and warm as Cashmere *dulai*, quilts. The rulers of Jaipur were the first to make peace and establish matrimonial alliances with the Moguls and escaped wanton destruction in long raging warfare. This allowed them to patronize arts–both performing and culinary. Jaipur boasts of its own school of *Kathak* dance and style of *khayal* singing. The tradition of another classical style, the *dhrupad*, is also strong. In more recent periods, Jaipur has won international renown for the skill of its blue-blooded polo players. Jaipur is the centre point of the Shekavati region. This Janus-faced city provides the gateway to the fertile plains of the rivers Ganga and Yamuna lying to the east, and has imbibed diverse cultural influences from the imperial court at Delhi as well as from its Rajput neighbour to the west. Dozens of *thikana* in this erstwhile princely state may be compared with the *taluka* in Avadh, each proud of its gastronomic legacy and tradition of lavish hospitality. The princely 'spread' that a gastronome can savour at Jaipur–both vegetarian and non-vegetarian–is truly cosmopolitan.

Some parts of Rajasthan have distinct personalities and culinary identities of their own. **The present edition contains a new section on the Cuisine of Kotah contributed by Maharao Brijraj Singh and Maharani Uttara Devi of Kotah.** Highly respected gourmets in their own right, the authors of this section have added vignettes of the history of Kotah with photographs of a picturesque landscape to augment their text.

Another part of Rajasthan that has a distinct personality and culinary identity of its own is Marwar or *marubhumi*, the 'desert land proper' comprising Jodhpur and its *thikana*. This is the homeland of the Marwari trading community, intrepid travellers and entrepreneurs par excellence. Many of India's leading industrialists belong to this strictly vegetarian community. The repast of these merchant princes is neither bland or frugal. It is rich in all senses of the word. Myriad delicacies are made with lentils, spiced imaginatively and then made palate-worthy by incorporating generous dollops of ghee. *Daal baati churma* may have been the staple in the past but today *paneer*, *mawa* and dried fruits and nuts embellish the recipes. The denizens of Jodhpur claim that more than 125 varieties of *mirchi bada* are made in their city and they challenge the Jaipurwalas to match the bite of their *mawa* or *pyaz kachauri*. The arid land does not have many fresh vegetables and the locals have learnt to cope with this chronic shortage by the most of what is available — *kair*, *sangri* and *kanda*. Besides these *subzis*, fenugreek seeds are used for delicious preparations.

The Jainas are an illustrious religious 'minority' in India who follow an even more stringent vegetarian code. They comprise an important segment of the local mercantile community. There are many Jaina pilgrimages in Rajasthan – Ranakpur, Dilwara and Mount Abu. These attract a very large number of devout visitors every year. The orthodox

Jaina repast eschews roots and tubers and this has inspired the family cooks to improvise and mimic the common delicacies enjoyed by others. A festive or celebratory Jain banquet can match any other spread in taste and eye appeal. Great emphasis is laid on cleanliness, purity of ingredients and ayurvedic wisdom.

These diverse influences have mingled in Rajasthan to evolve a wonderfully satisfying repast–robust and regal at the same time, blending effortlessly the simple with the sublime.

Contents

Dedication	v
Acknowledgements	vi
Introduction	vii
Jiggs Kalra and Pushpesh Pant	
Weights & Measures	xv

The Cuisine of Kotah

Kotah - the Citadel, the City and its surroundings by Maharao Brijraj Singh	K 3
Fish	
Machchi Jholdaar	K 9
Methi Dahi Machchi	K 10
Chicken	
Murgh Korma	K 11
Kaalaa Murgh	K 12
Meat (Mutton)	
Kakadi Jholdar Maans	K 13
Bina Ghee ka Keema	K 14
Soola	K 15
Kebab Dashrath Singh	K 16
Vegetables	
Tamatar ka Saag	K 17
Makki ka Saag	K 18
Hare Chane ka Saag	K 19
Malai Kofta	K 20
Accompaniments	
Makki ki Khichdi	K 21
Jowar ka Khichda	K 22
Kitti	K 23
Daal (Lentil)	
Moong Daal Mogar Kotah Style	K 24
Ghuntwa Daal	K 25
Sookhi Daal	K 26
Eggs	
Steamed Masala Andaa	K 27
Jholdar Andaa	K 28

RAITA (SAVOURY YOGHURT)
  Kismiss ka Raita   K 29
  Pyaaz ka Raita   K 30

ROTI (BREAD)
  Chimti Batiya   K 31
  Chakri Batia   K 32

COLD DRINKS/REFRESHMENTS
  Keri ki Aanch   K 33
  Aam ka Phajitha   K 34

DESSERTS
  Ande ka Halwa   K 35
  Hare Chane ka Halwa   K 36
  Gunja   K 37
  Laddoo   K 38

THE REGAL REPAST

  Achaari Andey   3
  Khad Murg   6
  Khad   7
  Murg Sheora-Natwara   8
  Murg ke Mokul   9
  Murg ke Sooley   10
  Shorbedaar Murg   11
  Bhunney Murg ke Pasandey   12
  Handiwale Murg ke Pasandey   13
  Khadhe Masaley ka Gosht   14
  Khadhe Masaley ka Murg   15
  Murg ki Chaamp   16
  Maas ki Kadhi   17
  Akhaa Aad Dhungaar   18
  Akhaa Peenda   19
  Laal Maas   20
  Maalgoba   21
  Maas ke Sooley   22
  Gol Maas Kaacher   23
  Safaed Mass   24
  Mewar ka Khaas Mass   25
  Adlah   26
  Makki ka Soweta   27
  Bharwaan Pasandey   27
  Chaamp Badaami   29
  Gobhi Rajwadi   30
  Bharri Harri Mirch ka Khaata   31

Paneer ke Sooley	32
Amrud ki Subzi	33
Scoop Lady Di	34

The Merchant Princes' Bhoj

Arbi ke Kebab	37
Jaipuri Subz Seekh	38
Aloo ki Tehree	39
Baingan Bemisaal	40
Baingan ki Launj	42
Bharwaan Parwal	43
Bhunney Bharre Badhi Mirch	44
Dhania Khumb Mongodi	45
Maaweywale Aloo	46
Malaai Kofta	47
Rasgulley ki Subzi	48
Chandrakaar Paneer	49
Muttar ki Kachori	50
Til ki Tikki Tamater ki Tari	51
Marua Aloo ke Saath	51
Mirchiwala Paneer	53
Paneer Jaipuri	54
Pudina Paneer	55
Keri ki Launjee	56
Makki ka Halwa	57

The Marwar Menu

Kandhey ki Subzi	61
Papad Methi ki Subzi	62
Bhunnee Besan ki Masaledaar Bhindee	63
Chatpatti Gobhi	64
Dhania Aloo Mongodi	65
Mongodi ki Subzi	66
Heeng Jeerey ke Aloo	67
Methi Kishmish	68
Mawa Muttar	69
Kadhi Pakorhi	70
Urad ki Daal	71
Besan ke Gatte	72
Moong Daal Khilma	73
Daal Baati Churma	74
Balushahi	76
Kalakand	77
Badaam Burfi	78

Weights & Measures

The recipes in this book were perfected in the metric measures. The quantities however are given in both metric and American measures. As it is difficult to exactly convert from one to the other, adjustments have been made ensuring that the taste would not vary in the slightest.

Fortunately, in Indian cooking a few extra grams of onions or ginger or tomatoes will not make much of a difference. Nor would a few extra millilitres of water. Nevertheless, whenever the recipe has demanded exactness, it has been provided. For example, the reader will occasionally come across something like 3 cups + 4 tsp.

The following chart should help with the conversions :

1 Gram	=	0.035	ounces
10 Grams	=	0.35	ounces
100 Grams	=	3.5	ounces
200 Grams	=	7.0	ounces

To convert grams into ounces, multiply the grams by 0.035.

To give convenient working equivalents, the metric measures have been rounded off into units of 5 or 25 *(see the following chart)*

Ounces	Grams	Nearest Equivalent	Conversion
1	28.35	28	20/30
2	56.70	57	50/60
3	85.05	85	75/90
4	113.40	113	100/120
5	141.75	142	150
6	170.10	170	175
7	198.45	198	200
8	226.80	227	225
9	255.15	255	250
10	283.50	284	275/290
11	311.85	312	300/325
12	340.20	340	350
13	368.55	369	375
14	396.90	397	400
15	425.25	425	425
16 or 1 lb	453.60	454	450

For more convenient conversions, the following chart will be useful :

1 tsp (teaspoon)	=	5g
2 tsp	=	10g
3 tsp	=	15g
1 Tbs (tablespoon)	=	15g
1 Tbs	=	3 tsp or ½ oz
¼ cup	=	4 Tbs or 2 oz
⅓ cup	=	5 Tbs + 1 tsp
½ cup	=	8 Tbs or 4 oz
⅔ cup	=	10 Tbs + 2 tsp
¾ cup	=	12 Tbs or 6 oz
1 cup	=	16 Tbs or 8 oz
1 cup (liquid measure)	=	237 ml
1 oz (dry measure)	=	28.35g
16 oz (liquid measure)	=	2 cups or 1 pint
2 pints (liquid measure)	=	4 cups or 1 quart

To convert the commonly used ingredients in this book, the following chart will be a convenient guide:

VEGETABLES

Coriander (chopped)	1 cup	60g
	1 Tbs	4g
Green Peas (Shelled)	1 cup	160g
Mint (Chopped)	1 cup	60g
	1 Tbs	4g
Mushrooms	1 cup	70g
Onions (Chopped, diced)	1 cup	170g
Potatoes (diced, cubes)	1 cup	150g
Tomatoes (Chopped)	1 cup	225g

LENTILS

All daals	1 cup	200g
All dry beans	1 cup	200g
All gram (White, Bengal, etc.)	1 cup	200g

CEREALS

Rice	1 cup	200g
Semolina	1 cup	200g

FLOUR

Atta (whole-wheat flour)	1 cup	120g
Cornflour	1 cup	80g
Gramflour	1 cup	150g
Flour or roasted *channa daal*	1 cup	150g
Flour (all purpose)	1 cup	125g
Breadcrumbs	1 cup	100g

DAIRY

Cheddar Cheese (grated)	1 cup	110g
Cream	1 cup	240ml
Milk	1 cup	240ml
Yoghurt	1 cup	225g
Hung Yoghurt	1 cup	260g

FATS & OILS

Desi Ghee or Clarified Butter	1 cup	225g	1 Tbs	15g
Ghee or Vegetable Fat	1 cup	200g	1 Tbs	12½ g
White Butter	1 cup	225g	1 Tbs	15g
Groundnut Oil	1 cup	220ml	1 Tbs	15ml
Mustard Oil	1 cup	220ml	1 Tbs	15ml

SUGAR & SPICE

Castor (confectioner's) sugar	1 cup	120g	1 Tbs	8g
Granulated Sugar	1 cup	200g	1 Tbs	12g
Ajwain	1 tsp	2.5g	1 Tbs	7.5g
Black Onion seeds (Kalonji)	1 tsp	3.3g	1 Tbs	10g
Black Peppercorns	1 tsp	3.3g	1 Tbs	10g
Coriander seeds	1 tsp	2g	1 Tbs	6g
Cumin seeds	1 tsp	3g	1 Tbs	9g
Fennel seeds	1 tsp	2.5g	1 Tbs	7.5g
Fenugreek seeds	1 tsp	4.5g	1 Tbs	13.5g
Kasoori Methi (Dry Fenugreek Leaves, broiled and powdered)	1 Tbs	12g		
Melon seeds	1 tsp	3.3g	1 Tbs	10g
Pomegranate seeds	1 tsp	3.3g	1 Tbs	10g
Poppy seeds	1 tsp	3g	1 Tbs	9g
Sesame seeds	1 tsp	3.5g	1 Tbs	10.5g
Sunflower seeds	1 tsp	3.3g	1 Tbs	10g
All powdered spices	1 tsp	5g		

DRY FRUITS & NUTS

Almonds (blanched, peeled)	1 cup	140g
Cashewnuts (peeled)	1 cup	140g
Coconut (grated)	1 cup	80g
Coconut (dessicated)	1 cup	60g
Peanuts (shelled, peeled)	1 cup	140g
Pistachio (blanched, peeled)	1 cup	140g
Raisins	1 cup	145g
Walnuts (chopped)	1 cup	120g

PASTES

Boiled Onion paste	1 cup	240g
Cashewnut paste	1 cup	250g
Coconut paste	1 cup	260g
Fried Onion paste	1 cup	265g
Garlic paste / Ginger paste	1¾ tsp	10g
	2½ tsp	15g
	4 tsp	25g
	5 tsp	30g
	3 tsp	50g

LIQUIDS

Lemon juice	1 cup	240ml
Water	1 cup	240ml

The Cuisine of Kotah

by
Maharao Brijraj Singh and Maharani Uttara Devi

Kotah - the Citadel, the City and its surroundings.

The City of Kotah is situated on the right bank of the river Chambal, at the centre of south eastern Rajasthan in the region known as Hadauti (the land at the Hadas). The Hadas are a major branch of the great Chauhan clan of the Agnikula Rajputs. They had settled in the hilly terrain near Bijolian at Bambaoda in the 12th century A.D. which became the capital of their hilly kingdom. The Hadas were feudatories of Mewar and extended their rule conquering Bundi in A.D. 1241 and Kotah in A.D. 1264. Some historians date both these events exactly 100 years later. The domain of the Hadas stretched from the hills of Bundi in the west to the Malwa plateaux in the east and to the south.

Hadauti is a fertile tract of land watered by several rivers with rich soil giving it a verdant look unlike the rest of Rajasthan. The largest and the only perennial monsoon fed river of Rajasthan, the Chambal (Charmanyavati) which flows through the land, finds mention in ancient texts like the Upanishads. It rises in the south and flows towards the north to join the river Jamuna. The river is geologically very old. The gorge ends near Kotah city.

Hadauti has been the abode of early man as is clearly evident from several well preserved Upper Paleolithic period cave paintings which date back to 20,000 B.C. Legend links it the epic periods of the Ramayana and Mahabharata. Being a fertile and prosperous area, it was the ancient battle ground between invading tribes like the Hoons (Huns) and the Sakas (Scythians) and the entrenched empires of ancient India like that of the Imperial Guptas and of Emperor Harsha Vardhana. During the medieval period, Hadauti attracted the attention of practically every powerful monarch of Delhi, for this region was one of the keys to the gates of Malwa and Gujarat. Numerous passages of arms, battles and sieges have left an imprint on this land. Nevertheless, scores of beautiful temples and countless treasures in sculpted stone are spread over miles in the wilderness; spectacular fortresses and grim strongholds, beautiful palaces, temples and delicate pavilions—all testify to a basic stability of society and its tradition and the continuity of culture, despite the military and political upheavals.

The building of Kotah city and the State began in A.D. 1264 when Prince Jait Singh of Bundi conquered this area and killed in battle the Bhil chieftain, Koteya. He raised the first battlements of the Garh (fort) by placing the head of the dead Koteya, as foundation stone, in the time honoured tradition of those days. Today, the Sailar Ghazi Darwaza rises at this spot. As the fort grew, a small settlement outside the walls also sprang up. It came to be called Kotah, after the dead Bhil chieftain. In due course the land and the state which later emerged in A.D. 1624 was also called Kotah.

The old town of Kotah was encircled and defended on three sides by a moat full of water and on the fourth side towards the west by the river Chambal, Massive crenellated walls with strong battlements and bastions formed two defence rings behind the moat. They were first erected by Rao Ram Singh in the 1690s and were later enlarged and strengthened when Zalim Singh was diwan. The actual work was executed by Dalel Khan, between A.D. 1790-1800. No stronger, thicker and higher city defence walls encircling a city exist anywhere except the famous walls of Theodosius in Constantinople (Istanbul). There were over 100 canons sited on the bastions to guard Kotah and they kept the city secure. It was never conquered. The famous Jwala Top, 18 ft. long, was the largest cannon forged in Kotah and can be seen outside the city wall near the Kishore Sagar lake.

Kishore Sagar, the picturesque man-made lake, adds beauty to Kotah. This lake or tank was built in 1346 A.D. by the Bundi Prince Dheer Deh. It is popularly called the Bada Talao. The island pavilion in it is called Jagmandir. It was build around A.D. 1740 by the Maharani Nrij Kunwar of Kotah. Below the bund is a the chhattra Bilas Garden, which is beautiful sight in spring with a profusion of flowers. A canal adorns the garden. The nearby Brij Bilas Palace today houses the Government Museum and the Art Gallery. The chattries of the Sar Bagh are on the other side. These *chattries* commemorate the memory of past Kings and have beautiful carvings and friezes. The rest of the area is a large public park with green lawns full of old trees. In the middle of the park is the Sri Umed Club built around 1890. A cricket grounds is in front of it. Next to this is the Maharao Umed Singh Stadium.

The English Cemetery, on the west, has graves of the English officers and civilians. It is well cared for by the Kota Heritage Society.

The Umed Park across the road has a magnificent bronze statue of H.H. Maharao Sir Umed Singh II (1889-1940) – the builder of modern Kotah. Among the many beautiful buildings, the pride of place after the Garh goes to Umed Bhawan Palace built in 1905. This was the modern residence of the Ruler of Kotah and was designed by Sir Swinton Jacob, RE., who made many other famous palaces and buildings in Rajasthan. It has been turned into a luxury hotel now and is managed by ITC Welcome-Heritage Group. Next comes Brijraj Bhawan, formerly the British Residency, built around 1840. It is now the residence of the present Maharao of Kotah besides being a Heritage Hotel. The Herbert College, now the Government College, built of white stone is another striking building. Opposite the Military Area built in the 1930s, with some of the best barracks for troops and houses for officers in the whole of India.

The old town of Kotah has many temples and havelis. The most famous temple is that of Mathureshji and the oldest one is Neelkanth Mahadeo, belonging to the 10th century A.D. Inside, near the Sabzi Mandi (vegetable market) are the tombs of Kesar Khan and Dokhar Khan, two Pathan brothers who had seized Kotah for a brief interlude between A.D. 1531-1551. Their yoke was thrown off by Rao Surjan of Bundi after a brief bloody battle.

On the river opposite the big Thermal Power Station is the Chambal Garden. This verdant spot provides a much needed place for citizens and children to enjoy fresh air and take in the view of the river. A boat service is also provided for people to take a short pleasure cruise on the river. As one progresses up-river the walls of the Chambal gorge rise higher. In the olden days one could see wild life including tiger, panther and sloth bear in comfort from the boat. The river was full of crocodiles and they could be seen basking on the sandbanks or on the rocks. By 1960 they were almost exterminated. Now, thanks to timely steps take to save them, they are making a come-back and can be viewed fairly regularly. Sadly there no tigers left to see.

The Chambal Barrage, a dam built to store water for irrigation, was built in 1960. With this, the level of the river has risen by over 120 ft. near the dam and so onwards upriver. Next to the Chambal Gardens is the famous Adhar Shila, a huge boulder slanting and appearing to fall in the river. Only this has not happened! The Amar Niwas, a pleasure palace built on the right bank of the river, now lies half submerged in the waters on account of the rising levels. The old Hanuman temple, now known as Godavari Dam and the Surya Mandir are close by. A favourite picnic spot for the locals is the Bhitariya Kund, with its 18th century A.D. Shivaling and the idol of a Panch Mukhi Ganesha.

Six miles (10 km.) east of Kotah, towards the industrial area, lies Kansuan Temple (Karneshwar Mahadeo). Legend has that is was the ashram of Kanva Rishi of ancient times and fame. A stone inscription dating back to A.D. 740 says it was built by Raja Shivgan Maurya. Beyond Kansuan another four miles away is Umed Ganj, with its twin lakes and a pleasure garden with a small palace and a pavilion in the middle of the lake. This was built by Maharao Umed Singh I (A.D. 1771-1819) Until the early 1950s there used be a dense forest around it where all kind of wild game was found including tiger and panther. The place abounded with cheetal deer.

Further down the road, two miles away is the ancient shrine of Dadh Devi Mata, which is still surrounded by a grove of old trees. A natural spring bubbles in the *kund* in front of the temple. Kaithoon village, the weaving centre where the world famous *Kotah Doria* sarees and cloth is made, is about four miles away. It has the only known temple dedicated to Vibhishan, the brother of Ravana, the Rakshas King.

The old Borkhandi Bridge, seven miles east of Kotah on themain highway to Gwalior dates to 1818. It was built by the British as a gift to the Kotah State for help rendered in the Pindari Wars. It is commonly known as Tod's Bridge, named after Col. James Tod.

To the west across the river Chambal lies Adhera Mahal, another pleasure palace built on the lake. In the olden days, it contained about 30-40 crocodiles and they were fed offal and would come on being called. Just below the bund of the lake is the small shrine of Karni Mata with a pretty garden. At nearby Nanta village stands the old palace of Jhala Zalim Singh who was the Diwan and later

Regent of Kotah State. The shrine of Kaal Bhairav dating back of the 14th century A.D is situated here.

The lovely temple of Keshorai Patan is situated on the bank of the Chambal, 7 miles to the north of Kotah. The chief temple of Shri Rangji was built by Rao Chhattar Sal of Bundi in A.D. 1653. Stone inscriptions dating to A.D. 35 and A.D. 93 exist nearby.

On the main highway to Jhalawar, 14 miles south of Kota is the village of Alnia. In the olden days there was good forest around here and it was famous for tiger *shikar*. Across the railway line, is an island in the Alnia stream, where one can walk across most of times. A group of rock shelters on it have lovely paintings of the Upper Paleolithic age dating back to 20,000 B.C. They are vivid and in good condition showing various animals and pre-historic man.

Towards the south on the road to Bardoli and Rawat Bhata Dam, 14 miles away is the big chasm of Gaiparnath, with a Shiv temple set deep inside the gorge. It offers a spectacular view of the forest and the rugged beauty of the cliffs of the Chambal valley. Further on about 10 miles away the road winds through the hills to the Mukund Darah Wild Life National Park, through the forested ghat section. The small cluster of the beautiful Bardoli Temples besides the road has some of the finest sculptures and architecture to be seen in Rajasthan, dating to 8th-9th century A.D. A miles further is the big Rawat Bhata Dam and the vast Rana Pratap Sagar. Across the lake is a nuclear power station. The big Bhainsrodgarh Fort rising sheer up from the cliff overlooking the river, dominates the fields and the valley with wooded hills encircling it.

The Mukund Darah Wild Life National Park, 35 miles south of Kotah, was once the most famous hunting preserve of the Kotah Kings. It was rich in flora and fauna. The range of Aravali hills enclose it runnings south-west to north-west. It is know as Darah; which means a pass, named after Rao Mukund Singh of Kotah. It is the only pass between the rivers Chambal and Kalishind between the rivers Chambal and Kalishind, a distance of 50 odd miles. Darah has an old palace and forifications, with the ruins of ancient Bhim Churi temples. The temple is linked to the legendary Bhimsen, the Pandav Prince of the Mahabharat era. A stone inscription dating to circa 450 A.D. tells us that a battle was fought here between the Hoons and the forces of Imperial Guptas.

Darah was the finest and famous shikargah of Kotah State, and the rulers hunted here from about A.D. 1630 upto the 1950s. The jungles, the hills, the cliffs and the wild tiger, boar and deer have all been vividly drawn and painted with rare artistry by the masters of the Kotah Kalam. The vast jungles sheltered even the wild buffalo and the rhino in the olden days up to the late 1700s as is evident from the paintings and old records. The jungles as painted are still visible quite unchanged! Only the plentiful wild life has disapperared—by unchecked poaching and the destruction of the forests.

Machchi Jholdar

Serves: 2
Cooking Time: 40 Minutes

INGREDIENTS

500 gms.	fish, cut into fillets
Salt to taste	
2 teaspoons	*haldi*
1½ cup	*tilli* oil for frying
1 teaspoon	*methi* seeds
2 tablespoons	onion paste
1 teaspoon	ginger paste
1 teaspoon	garlic paste
2 teaspoons	*dhaniya* powder
2 teaspoons	red chilli powder
4	green chillies, deseeded and slit half-way
	Few curry leaves
½ cup	thick tamarind water
1 cup	water or more
1	clove un-peeled garlic ⎫ pounded
1 teaspoon	*jeera* seeds ⎭ together

Season fish fillets with salt and *haldi* and keep aside for half an hour. Boil oil well till it smokes and subsides slightly. Fry fish, then remove the fish fillets from the oil. In the same oil fry the *methi* seeds till red (not black). Add the onion paste and fry till pinkish in colour. Add ginger paste and garlic paste and fry briefly. Add salt and and fry a bit. Add *dhaniya* powder, red chilli powder, green chillies and curry leaves and fry slightly.

Add tamarind water, water and fish fillets. Boil till curry thickens. Then add the unpeeled garlic and *jeera* seeds that have been pounded together. Keep on the fire for 2 to 3 minutes, then remove.

Note : The water can be varied according to the consistency needed.

Serve.

Methi Dahi Machchi

Serves: 3-4
Cooking Time: 40 Minutes

INGREDIENTS

½ kg.	fish, cut into biggish cubes
Few tablespoons oil	
2	onions, ground to a paste
1 cup or	fresh methi leaves,
5 teaspoons	dried *methi* leaves
2	green chillies
	Fresh (small bunch) *dhaniya leaves*
4-5	garlic cloves
	Small piece of ginger
1 cup	*dahi*, slightly sour
Pinch	*haldi* powder
1 teaspoon	*dhaniya* powder
1 teaspoon	sugar
2-3	tomatoes, scalded, skinned and chopped finely

In a biggish pan heat oil and fry fish a bit. Remove fish and keep aside. In the same oil fry the oion paste golden brown. Grind together *methi* leaves, green chillies, *dhania* leaves, garlic and ginger and blend into smoothly beaten *dahi*. When onions are ready, add *dahi* mixture to it and briefly cook. Then add *haldi* powder, *dhaniya* powder, sugar and tomatoes. Lower fire and cook for about 5-6 minutes. Now add fish, stir thoroughly, put lid on and cook till fish is ready (about 15 minutes). The *masala* will be thicker by now.

Serve.

Murgh or Mutton Korma

Serves: 4
Cooking Time: 1 Hours 30 Minutes

INGREDIENTS

1	medium chicken, jointed or
1kg.	mutton, cut into *botis*
300 gms.	oil
25	cloves
5	cardamoms
1 inch	cinnamon stick
2	bay leaves
500 gms.	onions, sliced
25 gms.	green chillies, de-seeded and slit halfway
50 gms.	ginger paste
4	garlic cloves paste
1 teaspoon	*haldi*
	Salt to taste
5 gms.	*dhaniya* powder
½ teaspoon	red chilli powder
50 gms.	cashewnut paste
100 gms.	*khus–khus* paste
500 gms.	*dahi*
¼	cup water

Boil oil well. Put a little aside. Add the cloves, cardamoms, cinnamon and bay leaves, and fry for a minute. Then add onion and green chillies and fry well. Add chicken or meat and fry for a while. Add ginger, garlic, *haldi* and salt, and cook till chicken or meat is fried well. Add *dhaniya* powder and fry for 5 minutes. Add red chilli power and fry slightly. Then add the oil that was kept aside. Half the cashewnut paste and half the *khus–khus* paste should be mixed in the *dahi* and kept aside. The rest of the cashewnut paste and *khus–khus* paste should be diluted in water and then added to the frying chicken or mutton. It should all be cooked till golden in colour. Add the *dahi* mixture and keep stirring (to avoid lumps). Cook till chicken or mutton is soft and ready and the curry is of required consistency.

Serve.

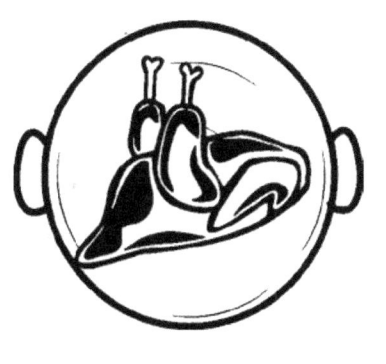

Kaalaa Murgh (Dark Fried Chicken)

Serves: 4
Cooking Time: 1 Hour

INGREDIENTS

1	medium chicken, jointed
300 gms.	onions (1 tablespoon chopped and the rest in paste)
3	garlic cloves (1 clove whole and the rest in paste)
2 teaspoons	*jeera*
250 gms.	oil
25 gms.	*khus–khus* paste
	Salt to taste
100 gms.	*dhaniya* powder
35 gms.	red chilli powder
30 gms.	ginger paste
15	cloves
1 inch	cinnamon stick
5	cardamoms
1 teaspoon	*haldi* powder
	Salt to taste

Mix the chicken well with all the ingredients except the 1 tablespoon of chopped onions, all the garlic clove and *jeera*. Add enough water and boil till it is done. Take out chicken pieces only, leaving *masala* aside. Boil the oil and fry chicken pieces for a while. Take out the pieces and keep aside. In the same oil put in chopped onion pieces and fry well. Add the kept aside *masala* and chicken and fry till dark, dry and done. Pound the clove of garlic with *jeera*, and add to the curry. Stir slightly and take the dish off the fire. There should be a bit of oil left in the *masala* of the curry after it is done.

Serve hot.

Kakadi Jholdar Maans

Serves: 4
Cooking Time: 1 Hours

INGREDIENTS

800 gms.	mutton diced into botis or
1	medium size chicken, jointed
2 teaspoons	ginger paste
	Salt to taste
2½ teaspoons	red chilli powder
½ teaspoon	*haldi* powder
3½ teaspoons	*dhaniya* powder
2 teaspoons	garlic paste
1½ teaspoons	*jeera* paste
3	cardamoms
	Oil for cooking (any oil)
8	cloves
1	inch piece cinnamon
2 cups	pieces of onions (medium cut)
1	big yellow cucumber or 2 medium ones, cut into 3 inch square pieces, skinned de-seeded with centre part removed
4	green chillies de-seeded and slit half-way
	Few curry leaves
1 cup	thin tamarind water
1 cup	water

On the meat pieces or chicken pieces smear the ginger, salt, red chilli powder, *haldi*, *dhaniya* powder, garlic and *jeera*, and put aside for a while. Heat the oil well, and put in it cardamoms, cloves and cinnamon. Fry for a while, then add the onion pieces. Let this too get fried, then put in *masala* smeared mutton pieces or chicken pieces. Fry mutton or chicken for a while, after which add the cucumber pieces, green chillies and curry leaves. Cover the vessel and cook on a slow fire. If the meat takes a while to cook, add a little water and cook till tender. Now add the tamarind water and water. Cook for a while. When the raw smell of tamarind goes away, remove it from fire. It is ready. If while cooking the *jholdar masala* becomes too thick, add sufficient water to bring it to the required consistency. Remember that this dish has a thinnish *jhol*.

Serve.

Bina Ghee ka Keema

Serves: 2
Cooking Time: 1 Hour

INGREDIENTS

500 gms.	*keema* (minced meat)
2 teaspoons	salt
1 teaspoon	*haldi* powder
125 gms.	*dhaniya* leaves, finely chopped
½ teaspoon	red chilli powder
10	garlic cloves coarsely chopped
375 gms.	onions, sliced
125 gms.	*dahi*, smoothly beaten
1 tablespoon	*jeera*
1½ tablespoons	Worcestershire sauce
	Few drops of *ghee*

Mix the *keema* with salt, *haldi, dhaniya* and red chilli powder and put them in a pressure cooker. Add enough water to just cover the *keema*. Cook for 5 to 7 minutes. Then add garlic and onions and cook till golden in colour. Add the *dahi* and cook till almost done. Just before fully cooked, add *jeera* and Worcestershire sauce and cook till it is ready. It will now be dry with all the water evaporated. Make an empty space in the middle of the *keema* and put in a live coal piece. Sprinkle a few drops of *ghee* on the coal for *Dhungar*, cover and leave for a few minutes. Serve.

Soola

Serves: 2
Cooking Time: 40 Minutes

INGREDIENTS

1 kg.	mutton or game meat – preferably leg
500 gms.	onion paste
300 gms.	garlic paste
100 gms.	ginger paste
50 gms.	*kaachri* paste
500 gms.	onion sliced for garnish
2 teaspoons	red-chilli powder
500 gms.	*dahi*
	Salt to taste
	Ghee or oil for basting – as needed

Cut meat into long thin fillets – approx 3" long and ½" wide. Mix in dish *dahi*, onion paste, garlic paste, ginger paste, *kaachri* powder, red-chilli powder and salt – all together nicely. Add cut meat fillets into this mixture and mix thoroughly by hand. Let all this marinate in dish overnight. Put dish in refrigerator, if it is summer.

Take a square-cut *soola* rod. A plain round rod is unsuitable, as the meat after a while starts slipping. On the rod pierce one large half-cut onion towards the handle and then slowly pierce the fillets, folding each fillet 2 or 3 times and then pushing then towards the handle. Keep piercing fillets till rod is full. Then pierce the other half-cut onion at the open end. Similarly pierce meat fillets on other rods as needed, till entire meat is on rods. With your hand cover the residue of *dahi* mixture over these *soolas* on rods nicely. Tie the meat all over the rod with a long thin string, so that all loose ends of meat hanging out, form one thick layer on the rod. This prevents meat from dropping into fire.

Bar-b-que the meat over open fire (live coals). The fire must not be too high – but glowing hot. The rod with *soolas* must be kept at least 6" above the fire. Every 5 minutes baste *soolas* with ghee or oil generously and also turning rod every five minutes. In around 15-20 minutes all the *soolas* shall start turning brown and get cooked. Prick with blunt tooth-pick to check if meat is done. If the tooth-pick goes in easily, the *soolas* are done. Remove from fire, untie the string while holding rods upright over a large *thali*. Then push out *soolas* gently, arrange in dish as required and garnish with golden fried onions.

Serve warm.

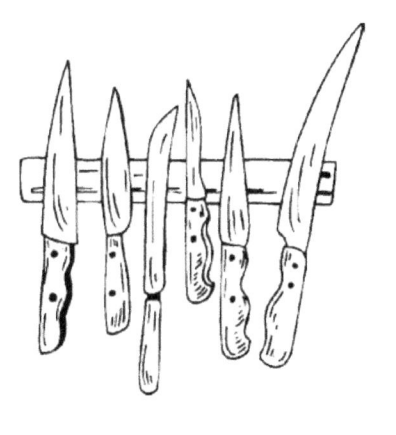

Kebab Dashrath Singh

Serves: 4-6
Cooking Time: 15 Minutes

INGREDIENTS

Makes approx 12 bite-sized kebabs

250 gms.	mutton or game meat
125 gms.	*chanaa daal*
5	cloves
2	*badi elaichi*
2	*choti elaichi*
2	bay leaves
2"	stick cinnamon
1 teaspoon	garlic paste
500 gms.	ginger paste
250 gms.	*ghee* or oil by weight
2	green chillies de-seeded slit half-way
20 gms.	green *dhaniya* leaves
1 teaspoon	red-chilli powder
10	black pepper – corns
2 teaspoons	salt
250 gms.	onions sliced and fried golden
1	egg
2 teaspoons	onions finely sliced
1 teaspoons	*amchoor* powder

This *kebab* is a recipe of Dashrath Singh, former cook in the royal household.

Make keema–meat. Mix this with *chanaa daal*, cinnamon, both *elaichis*, ginger paste, garlic paste, pepper–corns, bay leaves and red-chilli powder. Add enough water to cover this mixture and boil. When meat and *chanaa daal* are soft and cooked, (three should be no water left in pan) remove cinnamon stick and bay-leaves. Remove skins of both *elaichis* also. Add the *dhaniya* leaves, onions fried brown, finely sliced raw onions, green chillies chopped up, *amchoor* powder and salt. Break egg, mix it first and then add into this mixture and mix well with hand. Then grind everything on *silbatti* into a thick paste. Put this paste in a dish, make a clearing in middle and put a small live coal in the clearing. Pour ½ teaspoon of *ghee* over coal and cover dish for 5 min. to give *dhungar*. Take out and check taste for salt.

Make small 1" diameter *kebabs* for drinks and fry till golden. If making *kebabs* for a meal – make size bigger, say 1½" in diameter.

Serve warm.

Tamatar ka Saag

Serves: 4
Cooking Time: 20 Minutes

INGREDIENTS

500 gms.	tomatoes
1 tablespoon	oil
½ teaspoon	*jeera* seeds
1 tablespoon	onion paste
1 tablespoon	garlic paste
1 tablespoon	ginger paste
1 tablespoon	red chilli powder
1 tablespoon	*dhaniya* powder
	Pinch *haldi* powder
½ cup	water
2 teaspoons	sugar or jaggery crush
	Salt to taste

Boil some water and plunge tomatoes briefly into it, take them out and remove skins. Chop the tomatoes coarsely.

Heat oil in pan. Add to it the *jeera* seeds, stirring briskly, then put in onion paste, garlic paste and ginger paste. Stir fry for a minute or two. Now add red chilli powder, *dhaniya* powder, *haldi* powder and salt. Stir briefly, then add water. Let the *masala* cook well. Finally add the tomatoes and sugar or jaggery. Let it simmer and stir to blend well for a while. Taste for seasoning.

Serve.

Makki ka Saag

Serves: 4
Cooking Time: 30 Minutes

INGREDIENTS

500 gms.	corn kernels
2 tablespoons	oil
1 tablespoon	onion paste
1 tablespoon	garlic paste
1 tablespoon	ginger paste
1 tablespoon	red-chilli powder
1 tablespoon	*dhaniya* powder
	Salt to taste
2 cups	water

Cook the corn kernels in some water in pressure cooker till tender.

Heat the oil. Add to it the onion paste, garlic paste and ginger paste. Stir and cook for 2 to 3 minutes. Now put in red chilli powder, *dhaniya* powder, *haldi* powder and salt. Stir and cook till *masala* is well blended and cooked. Finally add the corn kernels and water. Cook for about 10 minutes. Adjust salt if necessary.

Serve.

Hare Chane (Boonta) ka Saag

Serves: 4
Cooking Time: 30 Minutes

INGREDIENTS

½ kg.	peeled green gram (*boonta*)
2 onions	diced small
½ teaspoon	garam masala
1½ teaspoon	red-chilli powder
½ teaspoon	*haldi* powder
½ tablespoon	*dhaniya* powder
100 ml.	*dahi*
2 teaspoons	garlic paste
3 teaspoons	onion paste
½ ginger	made in paste
4 tablespoons	oil
Salt to taste	

Put oil in wok and heat. Add diced onions and when golden add *garam masala* and peeled green-gram (*boonta*). Fry for 5 min. Add *haldi* powder and salt and cook on low heat. When nearly done add paste of onions, garlic, ginger paste and cook all together. When green-gram (*boonta*) is cooked and soft add red chilli powder and *dhaniya* powder. Cook till oil gets separated—then add *dahi* (well beaten) and mix thoroughly and cook on medium heat. Stir constantly. Keep cooking till oil separates. If more gravy is needed, add a little water and cook for 2-3 mins. Take out, garnish with chopped fresh *dhania* leaves and serve.

Malai Kofta

Serves: 6-8
Cooking Time: 1 Hour

INGREDIENTS

½ kg.	potatoes boiled and mashed
100 gms.	cashew-nuts split in halves
100 gms.	raisins
250 gms.	*maavaa*
500 gms. oil	to fry *Koftas*

For the gravy

2 tablespoons	oil
500 gms.	*dahi*
500 gms.	milk
250 gms.	*maavaa*
1 teaspoon	salt or to taste
½ teaspoon	*haldi* powder
½ teaspoon	salt
½ teaspoon	red-chilli powder
100 gms.	*maida* – to cover koftas
100 gms.	garlic paste
100 gms.	ginger paste
150 gms.	onion paste
1 tablespoon	*dhaniya* powder
2 tablespoons	red-chilli powder
½ teaspoon	*haldi* powder

Mix with mashed potatoes the *haldi* powder. red chilli powder and salt, and make small, approx 1" diameter, balls. Flatten the balls and add one tablespoon of *maava* cashew-nuts and raisins, all mixed together in the flattened balls and cover them up on all sides as round croquets. Roll the balls in *maida* and then deep fry them till golden. Keep aside.

Make gravy by heating one tablespoon oil in pan and add ginger paste, garlic paste and onion paste and heat for 5 minutes. Then add red chilli powder, *dahi* and cook for 5 minutes. Add milk. Cook for a minute and then add *maava* crumbled by hand. Cook for 5 minutes or heat over medium fire till gravy thickens.

Put *koftas* in serving dish and pour gravy over them and serve.

Makki (Kan) ki Khichdi

Serves: 4-6
Cooking Time: 00 Minutes

INGREDIENTS

6 corn cobs	with soft kernels
2 green chillies	slit, seeds taken out and finely chopped
¼ tbsp.	garlic paste
¾ tbsp.	onion paste
1½ teaspoon	red-chilli powder
½ tsp.	turmeric powder
½ tsp.	*garam masala*
150 ml.	*dahi*
2 tbsp.	oil/*ghee*
Salt to taste	

Take out corn kernels with a knife (as it is easier if they are soft). Fry the kernels in 2 tbsp. oil in a wok till golden. Then drain oil and keep separate. Grind the kernels coarsely after they have cooled.

Then put fresh 2 tsp. oil in wok and add garam masala, garlic, and onion paste, red chilli powder, turmeric powder and cook for 5 to 10 minutes. Add the corn kernels with dahi and green chillies and cook well. Add 2 cups of water and slowly cook till most of the water evaporates. Season with salt. Take out and serve, garnished with finely cut coriander leaves.

Jowar ka Khichda

Serves: 2
Cooking Time: 1 Hour

INGREDIENTS

100 gms.	jowar
300 ml.	water
250 ml.	milk
Salt to taste	
1 onion	paste
4 garlic cloves paste	
1 tablespoon	ghee
1 tablespoon	white butter

Put *jowar* in cold water for 1 hr. and wash thoroughly. Drain out and allow to dry completely for about 1½ hrs. Then put it in a *hamamdasta*, pound till all the skin etc. are separated. Throw away debris. The pounded *jowar* kernels should be well beaten to resemble crushed porridge. Heat *ghee* and add onion and garlic paste and cook till golden—not brown. Add the *jowar* and stir-fry for 5 mins. and cook 5-7 mins. more on slow fire. When *jowar* is soft and cooked and resembles porridge add white butter and stir cook for 5 mins.
Add salt to taste
Serve.

Methi Dahi Machi

Chimti Batiya

Chakri Batiya

Aam ka Phajitha

The Kotah Garh Palace

Jag Mandir Kishore Sagar, Kotah

Kitti

Serves: 3-4
Cooking Time: 30 Minutes

INGREDIENTS

250 gms.	*bajra atta*
100 gms.	*ghee*
250 gms.	milk
250 gms.	*dahi*
1 teaspoon	salt to taste

Heat the *ghee*. Put in the *bajra atta* and cook it until the colour changes. Add the milk and cook for 2 minutes, then add the *dahi* and salt, and cook for 5 minutes on a low flame, stirring constantly. When it gets a little thicker, check the seasoning.

Eat it along with non-vegetarian or vegetarian dishes. It goes especially well with *khato*, which is the Rajasthani word for *kadhi*.

Serve warm.

Moong Daal Mogar Kotah Style

Serves: 4
Cooking Time: 30 Minutes

INGREDIENTS

250 gms.	moong daal
2 or 3	medium onions sliced finely
4-6	green chillies de-seeded, sliced
4 tablespoons	oil
	Pinch haldi powder
½ teaspoons	garam masala powder
	Few curry leaves
	Salt to taste
Juice of 1 lemon	

Soak *moong daal* for ½ hrs. in cold water. Cook *daal* in water till each kernel is well cooked, separate and soft. Heat oil and fry green chillies for 2 mins. Do not allow to turn brown. Remove. Add in the same oil, onions and curry leaves. When onions turn golden, add *haldi, garam masala* powder and fried green chillies. Pour this mixture over the daal. Add salt and lemon juice. Mix properly, sprinkle green *dhaniya* leaves as garnish.

Serve.

Ghuntwa Daal

Serves: 6
Cooking Time: 1 Hour

INGREDIENTS

250 gms.	*daal moong mogar*
1 tablespoon	garlic paste
1 tablespoon	red-chilli powder
1 tablespoon	*haldi* powder
1 tablespoon	*ghee* or white butter
1½ litre	stock
1 tablespoon	salt or to taste
1 tablespoon	coriander powder
1	large pinch *garam masala*
1	large pinch *heeng*

Put *daal* in cold water for 1 hr. Then wash it 3 times in cold water and set aside in a colander, throwing out the water.

Heat *ghee* or butter in the pressure cooker, put *garam masala* and all other ingredients in it and fry for 2 or 3 minutes over medium heat. Add 2 cubes of Maggi Chicken Bullion in 1½ litres of water and heat to dissolve cubes in water to make stock. This can also be made by the usual method of using bones. Then add 1½ litre stock and *daal* and mix, stirring well. Cook under pressure on medium heat for 30-40 minutes. Open and check whether all *daal* is thoroughly mixed into a souplike mixture. Check for taste.

Serve hot.

Sookhi Daal

Serves: 4
Cooking Time: 30 Minutes

INGREDIENTS

250 gms.	*moong* or *masoor daal* washed. Soak in water for ½ hour
About 4 tablespoons oil	
4-6	green chillies, de-seeded and slit
2-3	onions, finely sliced
	Few curry leaves
	Pinch *haldi* powder
	Salt to taste
½ teaspoon	*garam masala* powder
	Juice of 1 lemon (optional)
	Dhaniya leaves, chopped for garnishing

Boil *daal*, just correct, neither undercooked nor mushy. This is crucial. Each kernel should be whole and separate. Set aside. Heat oil. Drop in the green chillies and fry till colour starts to change. Drain and keep aside for garnishing. In the same oil (add more if needed) put in onions and curry leaves and fry gently till golden. Add *haldi*, salt and cooked *daal*. Stir gently so that *daal* kernels do not break. Sprinkle the *garam masala* over this and stir in the lemon juice (optional). Gently mix. Garnish with fried green chillies and *dhaniya* leaves.

Serve.

Steamed *Masala Andaa*

Serves: 4
Cooking Time: 1 Hour

INGREDIENTS

6	eggs
6	onions (medium size), finely chopped or made to paste
6 teaspoons	*masala* paste made of 3 tsp. *dhaniya* paste
1½ tsp.	*jeera* paste and
1½ tsp.	ginger paste
4 teaspoons	of *khus-khus* made of 3 tsp. *khus-khus* and 1 tsp. copra paste
2 teaspoons	cashewnut paste
3	green chillies, de-seeded finely chopped
	A few *dhaniya* leaves
	Red-chilli powder, salt and *haldi* to taste
	Oil for frying
	A few *jeera* seeds
	A few curry leaves
2 tablespoons	onion paste
1½ cups	water

The eggs can be also steamed whole in the egg shells, in which case break the eggs as little as possible right at the top, and then preserve the egg shells.

Beat the eggs well, and mix the egg mixture thoroughly with half of the finely chopped (or paste) onions, 2 teaspoons of the *masala* paste, 2 teaspoons of the *khus-khus* and copra paste. 1 teaspoon of the cashewnut paste, finely chopped green chillies, a few *dhaniya* leaves, red-chilli powder, salt and *haldi*. This mixture can either be steamed in a pressure cooker for 10 to 15 minutes or put back into the empty egg-shells and the cracks or apertures sealed with *atta* to ensure there is no leakage during steaming. Steam for the same amount of time. Let it cool. If using the whole eggs in the shells, gently break the egg-shells and take out the whole egg. If using the egg mixture, steamed flat in a tray then cut the cake-like mixture into required sizes. Fry the whole eggs or cut eggs in a little oil, and keep aside.

Put about 4 tablespoons of oil in a frying pan, add a few *jeera* seeds and curry leaves, then add the remaining half of finely chopped (or paste) onions, and fry to a golden brown. Add the 2 tablespoons onion paste and fry, add the remaining *masala* paste and cook; add the balance *khus-khus* and copra paste, the left over cashewnut paste, a little salt, *haldi*, chilli powder and about ½ cups of water and fry for a few minutes. Add eggs (whole or cut) and fry till curry is brown and liquid evaporated.

Serve.

Jholdar Andaa

Serves: 4
Cooking Time: 30 Minutes

INGREDIENTS

6	eggs
150 gms.	oil
250 gms.	onions (one onion cut in big pieces, the rest in paste)
1 teaspoon	mustard seeds
1 teaspoon	methi seeds
4	green chillies, de-seeded and slit half way
3	curry leaves
3	garlic cloves, half a clove peeled, the rest in paste
10 gms.	ginger paste
½ teaspoon	*haldi* powder
50 gms.	red-chilli powder
	Salt to taste
50 gms.	tamarind to be made into 6 cups of tamarind water
2 teaspoons	*jeera*

Boil the oil. Hard-boil the eggs and shell them. Notch them and fry them in oil to golden colour. Put the eggs aside. In the same oil put in onion slices, mustard seeds and *methi* seeds and fry briefly. Then add green chillies, curry leaves, onion paste, garlic paste and ginger paste and fry. Add *haldi* powder, *dhaniya* powder and chilli powder and fry well. Put in salt and tamarind water and let it boil for a bit. Add eggs and let the curry boil till it thickens to required consistency. The half peeled garlic and *jeera* should be crushed together and added to the curry. Boil for a minute or two, then take it off the fire.

Serve.

Kishmish ka Raita

Serves: 2
Cooking Time: 15 Minutes

INGREDIENTS

4 tablespoons	*kishmish* (raisins)
2 cups	*dahi*, beaten smooth
1 teaspoon	roasted *rai* seeds
1 teaspoon	roasted *jeera* powder
¼ teaspoon	red-chilli powder
	Salt to taste
1 teaspoon	sugar
7	*pudina* leaves finely chopped

Soak the raisins (*kishmish*) in warm water till they fill up with water. Throw the water away. Now mix well together all the ingredients in strained *dahi*. Keep in a refrigerator till well chilled.

Serve cold.

Pyaaz ka Raita

Serves: 4-5
Cooking Time: 15 Minutes

INGREDIENTS

500 gms.	*dahi,* beaten
½ teaspoon	roasted *rai* seeds, coarsely powdered
½ teaspoon	red-chilli powder
½ teaspoon	roasted *jeera* seeds, coarsely powdered
½ teaspoon	salt, or to taste
3 tablespoons	castor sugar
3	onions, diced (not too small), or sliced if you prefer

Strain the *dahi*. Add all the ingredients and mix well. It will have a sweet and sour taste. Taste and adjust the seasoning accordingly. Chill well in the refrigerator.

Serve cold.

Chimti Batiya

Serves: 4-5
Cooking Time: 30 Minutes

INGREDIENTS

500 gms.	*atta*
200 gms.	*ghee*
100 gms.	water or as required
1 teaspoon	salt
200 gms.	*ghee* for soaking the *batiya*

Mix into *atta*, the ghee and salt. Then add as much water as required to make a proper firm dough. Leave it aside for 10 minutes. Divide the dough into individual patties or *loya*. Using a rolling pin, roll them out into thick *rotis* the size of *puris* (not too small). With your thumb and fore-finger pinch a design on top of the roti – any design e.g. cross shape, concentric circles etc. Heat a *tawa*, and roast the *batiyas* till golden brown on both sides. Once done dip the *batiyas* into the *ghee* kept in a shallow bowl to briefly soak them. Take them out, shake off the excess ghee, and keep aside warm to serve with food.

Chakri Batia

Serves: 4-5
Cooking Time: 30 Minutes

INGREDIENTS

500 gms.	atta
100 gms.	ghee
150 ml.	water
500 gms.	ghee or oil for frying batiya
½ teaspoon	salt

Sieve the flour, add *ghee* (100 gms.) and salt in it. Then mix water to this mixture to make a normal dough. It should be springy and firm. Make out 8 patties or *loyas*. With rolling pin make each patti or into circular thick *roti* : with a brush or finger grease top with ghee. Then fold the *roti*. It will be a folded piece of dough about 4" long. Then tightly make this folded piece of dough into spiral roll. Then with rolling pin again roll this spiral into a thick *roti* 4" in diameter. On a hot tawa put ghee or oil and shallow fry each roll on both sides till golden. The *batiyas* should be crisp and flaky.

Serve warm with food.

Keri ki Aanch

Serves: 4-5
Cooking Time: 30 Minutes

INGREDIENTS

1 kg.	raw mangoes
750 ml.	water
200 gms.	castor sugar
½ littre	extra water
1 teaspoon	red-chilli powder or to taste
1 teaspoon	salt to taste
1 teaspoon	roasted *jeera* seeds, coarsely powdered

Put the raw mangoes into 750 ml. water and remove the skins. Throw away skin and stones. Boil the mangoes until very soft. Cool completely. Strain the green mango liquid. Put in the remaining ½ litre water, castor sugar, chilli powder, salt and *jeera*. Mix well. It should have a sweet and sour taste. It will be a thin liquid, not thick. It makes a perfect summer drink.

Serve chilled.

Aam ka Phajitha

Serves: 4
Cooking Time: 30 Minutes

INGREDIENTS

4	mangoes
250 gms.	*dahi*
1 teaspoon	roasted *rai* seeds, coarsely ground
1 teaspoon	roasted *jeera*, coarsely ground
100 gms.	castor sugar
	Salt to taste
	Pinch red-chilli powder

Take out the juice from the mangoes. Set aside the mango-stones and strain the juice. Beat the *dahi* smooth and strain it in muslin cloth. Mix together the strained mango juice and strained *dahi*. Add to it the *rai* and *jeera*. Taste it, then add to it the castor sugar, salt and red-chilli powder. Put the mango stones back in the juice and chill well in the refrigerator. When ready to serve, place each mango stone in individual small bowls, pour mango juice over it and serve one bowl per person. It has a sweet and sour taste. The sugar and salt can be accordingly adjusted. It is an ideal summer refreshment.

Serve chilled.

Ande ka Halwa

Serves: 3
Cooking Time: 10 Minutes

INGREDIENTS

6 eggs	medium size Use one egg shell, after breaking off top as a measure
6 eggs	shells filled with *ghee*
6 eggs	shells filled with castor sugar

Break one egg slightly on the top so that the egg can be poured out. Keep the rest of the egg-shell intact and use it as a measure. If you are using six eggs, you will need six egg-shells filled with *ghee* and six egg-shells filled with sugar. The ratio is one egg, one egg-shell sugar and one egg-shell ghee i.e. 1-1-1.

Beat the eggs lightly so that yolks and whites are well mixed. Pour into this *ghee* and add sugar. Mix well. Put this mix in a *kadhai* and heat on low fire. Keep stirring continuously. Ensure that the flame is constantly low, not high. When the entire mixture resembles a soft scrambled egg, the *halwa* is cooked. It must not harden. Take the *kadhai* off the heat and continue to stir for a while. The cooking process takes about 10 to 15 minutes.

Serve warm.

Hare Chane ka Halwa

Serves: 5-6
Cooking Time: 40 Minutes

INGREDIENTS

500 gms.	fresh green gram peeled
375 ml.	*ghee* by weight
450 gms.	milk by weight
500 gms.	sugar

Finely grind the peeled green gram. Put the ground green gram and *ghee* in a *kadhai* and heat. Ensure flame is low and cook well. When *ghee* separates from green gram, add milk. Continue to stir and cook until milk is completely absorbed and not visible. Then add sugar. Continue to stir and cook for a while on a low flame till sugar has completely dissolved. Then take it off the fire. The ghee will have separated from the green gram and the gram will have sunk to the bottom of the *kadhai*. Mix well.

Serve.

Gunja

Serves: 6-8
Cooking Time: 1 Hour 30 Minutes

INGREDIENTS

500 gms.	*maida* (flour)
250 gms.	*maavaa*
200 gms.	roasted *sooji*
250 gms.	sugar powder
200 gms.	*khopra giri*
1 litre oil	for frying

Sieve *maida* flour and add cold water to make a dough. Set aside for 15 minutes. Mix well in bowl, *maavaa*, sugar powder, *khopra giri* and *sooji*. Set aside. Make 12-16 balls or *loya* of dough with rolling pin. Make flat round pieces and then put each piece in a *gunja* mould. Put in this the mixture of *maavaa*, sugar, *khopra giri* and *sooji* and press well. Cover the *gunja* mould with mixture on top with another flat piece of dough. Wet the edges of both flat dough pieces in the mould and on top and seal edges. Carefully lift out each stuffed *gunja* piece and place on tray. In a *wok* or *kadhai* heat oil on medium heat and deep-fry *gunja* pieces till light brown or golden. Set aside on tray and let cool.

Serve with cold cream.

Laddoo

Serves: 6-8
Cooking Time: 2 Hour

INGREDIENTS

500 gms.	atta
100 gms.	ghee for atta
10 pieces	small elaichi (skin removed)
200 gms.	milk or more if needed

Mix *atta* with the 100 gms. *ghee* and mix well. Slowly add milk into the *atta* to make a dough. Make 8-10 pattis or *loyas* out of this dough by hand. Put these balls in a hot oven and when well cooked or light-brown colour remove. After cooling, grind well on *sil-batti* till granulated. Then add to this the rest of the sugar and *elaichi*. Then with hand roll this mixture into medium sized *laddoos*, pressing into shape. Place on a in dish and serve.

The Regal Repast

Achaari Andey

Serves: 4
Preparation Time: 1 hour
Cooking Time: 25 minutes

INGREDIENTS

8	Eggs (hard boil, cool, shell & prick with a fork)
120ml/½ cup	Mustard Oil
2	*Lavang*/Cloves
1	*Daalcheeni*/Cinnamon (1")
2	*Tej Patta*/Bay Leaf
1.25g/½ tsp	*Shahi Jeera*/Black Cumin Seeds
	A generous pinch of *Kalonji*/Black Onion Seeds
	A small pinch of *Methidaana*/Fenugreek Seeds
1.5g/½ tsp	*Chhotti Elaichi*/Green Cardamom Powder
1.5g/½ tsp	Black Pepper (freshly roasted & coarsely ground)
0.75g/¼ tsp	*Lavang*/Clove Powder
0.375g/⅛ tsp	*Daalcheeni*/Cinnamon Powder
0.375g/⅛ tsp	*Javitri*/Mace Powder
0.5g/1 tsp	*Kesar/Zaafraan*/Saffron

The Onion Masala

100g/3 oz	Onions (grind to a paste)
10g/1¾ tsp	Garlic Paste (strain)
4.5g/1½ tsp	Red Chilli Powder
1.5g/½ tsp	*Haldee*/Turmeric Powder
	Salt

The Almond Paste

16	Almonds (soak overnight and peel)
45ml/3 Tbs	Lemon Juice

PREPARATION

THE ONION MASALA: Put all the ingredients in a bowl and mix well.

THE ALMOND PASTE: Grind almonds with lemon juice, ideally with a *sil-batta*, else in a grinder/processor.

COOKING

Heat oil in a *kadhai*/wok, add cloves, cinnamon, bay leaf and black cumin seeds, stir over medium heat for a few seconds, add onion masala and *bhunno*/stir-fry until light golden. Then add almond paste, *bhunno*/stir-fry for a minute, add eggs, stir carefully, add *kalonji* and fenugreek, and cook for a minute. Now add cardamom, pepper, clove, cinnamon and mace powders, stir for a few seconds, add saffron, stir, remove, adjust the seasoning, cover and keep warm for a few minutes before serving.

Note: To preserve it as a pickle, increase the quantity of oil by 60ml/¼ cup and allow it to mature for 4-5 days.

Methi Machchi

Serves: 4
Preparation Time 30 minutes
Cooking Time 25 minutes

INGREDIENTS

1kg/2¼ lb	Sole/Sea Salmon/*Surmai*/*Gole* (2½" cubes)

The Marination

90ml/6 Tbs	Lemon Juice
30ml/2 Tbs	Cooking Oil
6 flakes	Garlic (finely chop)
2.25g/¾ tsp	Red Chilli Powder
	Salt

The Gravy

60ml/¼ cup	Cooking Oil
1g/¼ tsp	*Methi*/Fenugreek Seeds
150g/5 oz	Onions (grate)
30g/5 tsp	Garlic Paste (strain)
15g/2½ tsp	Ginger Paste (strain)
250g/9 oz	Yoghurt
9g/1 Tbs	*Dhania*/Coriander Powder
4.5g/1½ tsp	Red Chilli Powder
3g/1 tsp	*Haldee*/Turmeric Powder
	Salt
1 litre/4¼ cups	Clear Fish Stock (or water)
15ml/1 Tbs	Lemon Juice
	A generous pinch *Kasoori Methi*

PREPARATION

THE MARINATION: Mix all the ingredients, evenly rub the fish cubes with this marinade and reserve for 15 minutes.
THE FISH: Arrange on a greased roasting tray and cook in a pre-heated (275°F) oven for 3-4 minutes.
THE YOGHURT: Whisk in a bowl, add coriander, red chillies and turmeric, whisk until incorporated.

COOKING

Heat oil in a *handi*/pan, add fenugreek seeds, stir over medium heat until they begin to pop, add onions, sauté until translucent and glossy, add the garlic and ginger pastes, *bhunno*/stir-fry until the onions are light golden. Remove *handi*/pan from heat, stir-in the yoghurt mixture and salt, return *handi*/pan to heat and *bhunno*/stir-fry until specks of fat begin to appear on the surface. Now add fish stock, bring to a boil, reduce to low heat and simmer until reduced by one third. Remove and pass the gravy through a fine mesh soup strainer into a separate *handi*/pan. Return the gravy to heat, bring to a boil, reduce to low heat, add the cooked fish and simmer for 1-1½ minutes. Now add lemon juice, stir, remove and adjust the seasoning. Crush *kasoori methi* between the palms, sprinkle and stir carefully. The gravy should be of thin sauce consistency.

TO SERVE

Remove to service bowl and serve with steamed rice.

Talli Machchi

Serves: 4

Preparation Time 30 minutes

Cooking Time 3-4 minutes

INGREDIENTS

12 fillets	Pomfret (60g/2 oz each)
To coat	*Rawa* / Semolina
	Cooking Oil to deep fry

The Coating

120g/4 oz	Onions (grate)
6 flakes	Garlic (finely chop)
5g/½" piece	Ginger (finely chop)
9g/1 Tbs	*Dhania* / Coriander Power
6g/2 tps	*Jeera*/Cumin Powder
6g/2 tps	Red Chilli Powder
	Salt
60ml/Ŏ cup	Vinegar

The Egg Dip

4	Egg Whites
A few sprigs	*Sua/Soya*/Dill (chop)

PREPARATION

THE COATING: Mix all the ingredients with vinegar in a bowl, evenly coat the fish with this mixture and reserve for 15 minutes.

THE EGGS: Put egg whites in a bowl, add soya, beat and keep aside.

COOKING

Heat oil in a frying pan, dip the fillets in the beaten eggs, roll in semolina and deep fry 3 or 4 fillets at a time over medium heat for 3-4 minutes or until semolina is crisp. Remove to absorbent paper to drain excess fat.

Khad Murg

Serves: 4
Preparation Time 2:15 hours
Cooking Time 1 hour

INGREDIENTS

2	Chicken (500g/1 lb 2 oz)
3	*Chhotti Elaichi*/Green Cardamom
2 sticks	*Daalcheeni*/Cinnamon (1")
2	*Motti Elaichi*/Black Cardamom
2	*Lavang*/Cloves
2	*Tej Patta*/Bay Leaf
480 ltr/2 cups	Clear Chicken Stock
12	Roomali Roti

The Marination

150g/5 oz	*Chakka Dahi*/Yoghurt Cheese/Hung Yoghurt
60g/5 Tbs	*Desi Ghee*/Clarified Butter
45g/1½ oz	Almond Paste
45g/1½ oz	Garlic Paste (strain)
30g/5¼ tsp	Ginger Paste (strain)
9g/1 Tbs	Red Chilli Powder
60ml/¼ cup	Lemon Juice
	Salt
1g/2 tsp	*Zaafraan*/Saffron
3g/1 tsp	*Chhotti Elaichi*/Green Cardamom Powder
1.5g/½ tsp	*Javitri*/Mace Powder
0.75g/¼ tsp	*Gulaab Pankhrhi*/Rose Petal Powder

PREPARATION

THE CHICKEN: Clean, remove the neck and the skin, prick the entire surface with a fork.
THE MARINATION: Mix all the ingredients, evenly rub the chicken with this marinade and reserve for at least an hour (preferably overnight in the refrigerator).
THE SAFFRON: Crush saffron threads with a pestle or the back of a spoon, reserve in 30ml/2 Tbs of lukewarm water for 20 minutes, and then make a paste.
THE OVEN: Pre-heat to 250°F.

COOKING

Arrange the chicken in a large *handi*/pot, leaving space between each bird, pour on the stock, add green cardamom, cinnamon, black cardamom, cloves and bay leaf, bring to a boil, reduce to low heat, cover and simmer for 20 minutes. Uncover and cook the chicken, basting at regular intervals with the *jus* until cooked and the stock completely absorbed. Remove and keep aside. Reserve the *roghan*.

THE FINISHING

Spread 6 *Roomali Roti*, overlapping (they should form a diameter big enough to wrap the chickens 'snugly'), on a work surface/table and spread half the *roghan* on the *roti*. Rub the chicken with saffron, place in the middle of the spread *roti* and wrap, tucking in the overlapping *roti*. Repeat the process for the remaining chicken and place both in a greased roasting tray.
Place the tray in the pre-heated oven and bake for 15 minutes.

TO SERVE

Unwrap the chicken at the table, carve and serve with onion rings and lemon wedges.

Khad

Serves: 4
Preparation Time 30 minutes
Cooking Time 1 hour

INGREDIENTS
800g/1¾ lb	Lamb Mince
300g/11 oz	Potatoes
120g/⅔ cup	Ghee
350g/12 oz	Onions
100g/3½ tsp	Yoghurt
20g/3½ tsp	Ginger paste
20g/3¼ tsp	Garlic paste
20g/4 tsp	*Dhania*/Coriander powder
5g/1 tsp	Red Chilli powder
3g/½ tsp	*Haldee*/Turmeric
	Salt
20g/¼ cup	*Dhania*/Coriander
4	Green Chillies
15ml/1 Tbs	Lemon juice
12	*Phulka* (Thin)

PREPARATION

THE VEGETABLES: Peel, wash and dice potatoes. Peel, wash and chop 100g/4 oz of onions; roughly cut the rest, put in a blender and make a rough paste. Clean, wash and chop coriander. Remove stems, wash, slit, deseed and finally chop green chillies.

THE MINCE: Whisk yoghurt in a large bowl, add the mince, the onion, ginger and garlic pastes, coriander powder, red chillies, turmeric and salt, mix well and keep aside for 10 minutes.

THE OVEN: Pre-heat to 270ºF.

COOKING

Heat ghee in a *kadhai*, add the the chopped onions and sauté over medium heat until golden brown. Reduce to low heat, add the mince mixture and *bhunno* for 5 minutes. Then add potatoes and *bhunno* until cooked and the liquid has evaporated (add a little water if necessary). Remove, add coriander and green chillies, stir. Sprinkle lemon juice and stir. Divide into 11 equal portions.

FINISHING

Prepare the 'cake' as follows: Spread a portion of the cooked mince on a *Phulka*. Please the second *Phulka* on the mince and spread another portion of the cooked mince, and so on until all the *Phulka* are stacked one on top of the other. Wrap the stack in greased silver foil, place on a baking tray and bake in the pre-heated oven for 8-9 minutes. Remove, turn over and bake for 8-9 minutes.

TO SERVE

Tear off the foil, cut into wedges of desired size and serve with *Kachumbar*, Mint Chutney and lemon wedges.

Note : *Khad* can be made in single *Chappati* rolls or balls. Divide the mince into 12 equal portions and wrap in individual *Chappati* and then in foil.

Murg Sheora-Natwara

Serves: 4
Preparation Time 45 minutes
Cooking Time 20 minutes

INGREDIENTS

1 Kg/2¼ lb	Chicken *Tikka* (1½" pieces from the leg)
100g/½ cup	*Desi Ghee*/Clarified Butter
5	*Chhotti Elaichi*/Green Cardamom
4	*Tej Patta*/Bay Leaf
12	Black Peppercorns
150g/5 oz	Onions (finely chop)
8 flakes	Garlic (finely chop)
10g/1" piece	Ginger (finely chop)
250ml/9 oz	Yoghurt
4.5g/1½ tsp	*Dhania*/Coriander Powder
	Salt
25g/½ cup	*Taaza Dhania*/Coriander (chop)
17.5g/½ cup	*Taaza Pudhina*/Mint (finely chop)
12	Green Chillies (seed & finely chop)
0.75g/¼ tsp	*Jaiphal*/Nutmeg Powder
4	Fresh Red Chillies (seed & cut into strips)

PREPARATION

THE YOGHURT MIXTURE: Put yoghurt in a bowl, add coriander powder and salt, and whisk to mix well.

COOKING

Heat *ghee* in a *handi*/pan, add cardamom, bay leaf and peppercorns, stir over medium heat until the cardamom begins to change colour, add onions, garlic and ginger, and sauté until translucent and glossy. Then add chicken, increase to high heat and *bhunno*/stir-fry to sear (approx 3-3½ minutes). Remove *handi*/pan from heat, stir in the yoghurt mixture, return *handi*/pan to heat, add the remaining ingredients and water (approx 240 ml/1 cup), cover with a lid, seal with *atta* dough, reduce to low heat and cook, shaking the *handi*/pan at regular intervals, for 7-8 minutes. Remove, uncover, stir well and simmer for 2-3 minutes or until the gravy is thick. Remove and adjust the seasoning.

Murg Ke Mokul

Serves: 4

Preparation Time
30 minutes

Cooking Time
20 minutes

INGREDIENTS

800g/1lb 13 oz	Chicken Breasts (bone & cut into ½" thick strips)
60g/5 Tbs	*Desi Ghee*/Clarified Butter
5	*Lavang*/Cloves
4	*Chhotti Elaichi*/Green Cardamom
10	Black Peppercorns
2	*Tej Patta*/Bay Leaf
2 blades	*Javitri*/Mace
150g/5 oz	Onions (chop)
45g/2½ Tbs	Garlic Paste (strain)
30g/5 tsp	Ginger Paste (strain)
6g/2 tsp	*Dhania*/Coriander Powder
3g/1 tsp	*Haldee*/Turmeric Powder
2.25g/¾ tsp	Red Chilli Powder
150g/5 oz	Boiled Onion Paste
30g/1 oz	Cashew Nut Paste
30ml/2 Tbs	*Malaai*/Clotted Cream
220g/1 cup	Yoghurt (whisk)
	Salt

COOKING

Heat *ghee* in a *handi*/pan, add cloves, green cardamom, pepper, bay leaves and mace, stir over medium heat until the cardamom changes colour, remove the whole spices, add onions, sauté until translucent and glossy, add garlic and ginger, *bhunno*/stir-fry until the onions are light golden. Then add coriander, turmeric and red chilli powders (dissolved in 60ml/Ŏ cup of water), *bhunno*/stir-fry until specks of fat begin to appear on the surface, add boiled onion paste, and *bhunno*/stir-fry until specks of fat begin to appear on the surface. Add cashew nut paste, *bhunno*/stir-fry until specs of fat begin to appear on the surface, add chicken and cream, *bhunno*/stir-fry for 4-5 minutes. Remove *handi*/pan from heat, stir-in yoghurt, return *handi*/pan to heat, bring to a boil, reduce to low heat, cover and simmer, stirring occasionally, until the chicken is cooked and the gravy is of a sauce consistency. Remove and adjust the seasoning.

TO SERVE

Remove to a bowl and serve with *Roti* or *Phulka*.

Murg ke Sooley

Serves: 4
Preparation Time 1:30 hours
Cooking Time 20 minutes

INGREDIENTS

16	Piccata of Chicken (from the breast; 45g/1½ oz each)
	Desi Ghee/Clarified Butter to fry

The Marination

30g/1 oz	Roasted Almond Paste
30g/1 oz	Khoya
10g/1¾ tsp	Taaza Dhania/Coriander Paste
30g/5 tsp	Ginger Paste (strain)
20g/3¼ tsp	Garlic Paste (strain)
4.5g/1½ tsp	Red Chilli Powder
60g/¼ cup	Chakka Dahi/Yoghurt Cheese/Hung Yoghurt
15ml/1 Tbs	Lemon Juice
45g/1½ oz	Fried Onion Paste
3g/1 tsp	Amchoor/Mango Powder
3g/1 tsp	Black Pepper Powder (freshly roasted & coarsely powdered)
1.5g/½ tsp	Chhotti Elaichi/Green Cardamom Powder
0.75/¼ tsp	Lavang/Clove Powder
0.75/¼ tsp	Daalcheeni/Cinnamon Powder
0.75/¼ tsp	Javitri/Mace Powder
0.75/¼ tsp	Kebab Cheeni Powder

The Smoking

2	Chhotti Elaichi/Green Cardamom (split open)
4.5g/1 tsp	Desi Ghee/Clarified Butter

PREPARATION

THE MARINATION: Mix all the ingredients, in a bowl, evenly rub the piccata with this marinade and reserve for 1 hour.

THE SMOKING: Put a few small pieces of 'live' charcoal in a small *katori*/metal bowl and place the *katori*/metal bowl in a large *handi*/pan. Spread the *sooley* around the *katori*/metal bowl, place cardamom on the charcoal, pour on the *ghee* and, as the smoke bellows, cover with a lid and reserve for 15 minutes.

THE SKEWERING: Uncover, remove the *katori*/metal bowl, carefully skewer *sooley* in convenient batches, penetrating the meat twice, on thin skewers and the spread to ensure minimum curling.

COOKING

Roast on a moderately hot charcoal grill for 6-7 minutes, basting at regular intervals.

TO SERVE

Unskewer *sooley*, arrange on platter and serve hot.

Shorbedaar Murg

Serves: 4

Preparation Time
45 minutes

Cooking Time
30 minutes

INGREDIENTS

12	Chicken Drumsticks
75g/6 Tbs	*Desi Ghee*/Clarified Butter
6	Black Peppercorns
3	*Chhotti Elaichi*/Green Cardamom
2	*Lavang*/Cloves
1 stick	*Daalcheeni*/Cinnamon (1")
2	*Tej Patta*/Bay Leaf
3g/1 tsp	*Jeera*/Cumin Seeds
300g/11 oz	Onions (grate)
25g/4 tsp	Ginger Paste (strain)
15g/2½ tsp	Garlic Paste (strain)
6g/2 tsp	*Dhania*/Coriander Powder
4.5g/1½ tsp	Red Chilli Powder
3g/1 tsp	*Haldee*/Turmeric Powder
15g/2 Tbs	*Kopra*/Desiccated Coconut
	Salt
2	Tomatoes (thin roundels)
120g/4 oz	Yoghurt (whisk)
60g/2 oz	*Malaai*/Clotted Cream
4	Green Chillies (seed & cut in to strips)
1.5g/½ tsp	*Chhotti Elaichi*/Green Cardamom Powder
0.75g/¼ tsp	*Javitri*/Mace Powder
0.375g/⅛ tsp	*Gulaab Pankhrhi*/Rose Petal Powder

COOKING

Heat *ghee* in a *handi*/pan, add peppercorns, green cardamom, cloves, cinnamon, bay leaves and cumin, stir over medium heat until the cumin begins to pop, add onions, *bhunno*/stir-fry until translucent and glossy, add garlic and ginger, *bhunno*/stir-fry until the moisture evaporates. Then add coriander, red chillies, turmeric, salt and coconut (dissolved in 60ml/¼ cup of water), *bhunno*/stir-fry until the moisture evaporates. Add chicken, *bhunno*/stir-fry until specks of fat begin to appear on the surface, add tomatoes, and *bhunno*/stir-fry for a minute. Remove *handi*/pan from heat, stir-in yoghurt, return *handi*/pan to heat, *bhunno*/stir-fry until fat leaves the sides, add cream and green chillies, *bhunno*/stir-fry until fat leaves the sides again. Now add 480 ml/2 cups of water, bring to a boil, reduce to low heat, cover and simmer until chicken is cooked (approx 5 minutes). Sprinkle the powdered spices, stir, remove and adjust the seasoning.

TO SERVE

Remove to a service dish, garnish with coriander, sprinkle pepper and serve with *Phulka*, *Khameeri Roti* or *Roomali Roti*.

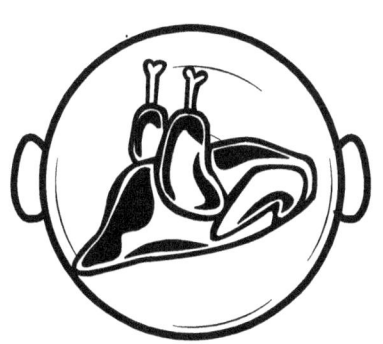

Bhunney Murg ke Pasandey

Serves: 4
Preparation Time 1:15 hours
Cooking Time
In the *tandoor*
2-3 minutes
In the oven
3-4 minutes

INGREDIENTS

6	Breasts of Chicken (120g/4 oz each)

The Marination

125g/½ cup	Yoghurt
30ml/2 Tbs	Lemon Juice
20g/3½ tsp	Garlic Paste (strain)
20g/3½ tsp	Garlic Paste (strain)
3g/1 tsp	Yellow Chilli Powder
3g/1 tsp	*Haldee*/Turmeric Powder
0.5g/1 tsp	Saffron
	Salt

The *Bhunnao*

75g/2½ oz	*Desi Ghee*/Clarified Butter
45g/1½ oz	*Besan*/Gramflour
0.75g/¼ tsp	*Shahi Jeera*/Black Cumin Seeds
2.25g/¾ tsp	*Chhotti Elaichi*/Green Cardamom Powder
1.5g/½ tsp	Black Pepper Powder
0.75g/¼ tsp	*Motti Elaichi*/Black Cardamom Powder
0.75g/¼ tsp	*Javitri*/Mace Powder
0.75g/¼ tsp	*Jaiphal*/Nutmeg Powder
0.75g/¼ tsp	*Kebab Cheeni* Powder
0.75g/¼ tsp	*Pathar ke Phool* Powder

PREPARATION

THE CHICKEN: Clean, bone, wash and pat dry. With a sharp knife, cut each breast into half horizontally.

THE MARINATION: Whisk yoghurt in a large bowl. Crush saffron flakes with a pestle or back of a spoon, reserve in lukewarm water for 15 minutes, and then make a paste. Mix saffron and the remaining ingredients with yoghurt, rub the chicken with this marinade and reserve in the bowl for 45 minutes.

THE *BHUNNAO*: Heat ghee in a frying pan, add *besan*, *bhunno*/stir-fry over medium heat until it emits its unique aroma, add *shahi jeera*, stir, add the marinated chicken, along with the marinade, and *bhunno*/stir-fry until the chicken is half cooked (approx 1½-2 minutes). Remove, sprinkle the spices, stir, cool and adjust the seasoning.

THE SKEWERING: Thread the skewer through the chicken supremes twice and then "spread" them as much as possible along the skewer to "flatten".

THE OVEN: Pre-heat to 350°F.

COOKING

Roast in a moderately hot tandoor for approximately 8-10 minutes. In the pre-heated oven, for 3-4 minutes.

TO SERVE

Arrange 3 *paarchey* on each of 4 individual plates and serve as a starter with sesame seed chutney.

Serves: 4

Preparation Time
1:30 hours

Cooking Time
30 minutes

Handiwale Murg ke Pasandey

INGREDIENTS

12	Chicken Thighs
	Desi Ghee/Clarified Butter to fry

The Marination

30g/1 oz	*Taaza Dhania*/Coriander Paste
20g/3¼ tsp	Ginger Paste (strain)
15g/2½ tsp	Garlic Paste (strain)
10g/1¾ tsp	Green Chilli Paste
45g/1½ oz	*Chakka Dahi*/Yoghurt Cheese/ Hung Yoghurt
45ml/3 Tbs	Lemon Juice
3g/1 tsp	Black Pepper Powder (freshly roasted & coarsely powdered)
1.5g/½ tsp	*Chhotti Elaichi*/Green Cardamom Powder
0.75/¼ tsp	*Lavang*/Clove Powder
0.75/¼ tsp	*Daalcheeni*/Cinnamon Powder
0.75/¼ tsp	*Javitri*/Mace Powder
0.75/¼ tsp	*Kebab Cheeni Powder*
	Salt

The Mince

400g/14 oz	*Kheema*/Chicken Mince
75ml/6 Tbs	*Desi Ghee*/Clarified Butter
4 flakes	Garlic (chop)
100g/3 oz	Onions (chop)
10g/1" piece	Ginger (chop)
4	Green Chillies (seed & chop)
9g/1 Tbs	*Dhania*/Coriander Powder
4.5g/1½ tsp	Red Chilli Powder
1.5g/½ tsp	*Haldee*/Turmeric Powder
4	Tomatoes (large; chop)
	Salt
1.5g/½ tsp	*Chhotti Elaichi*/Green Cardamom Powder
0.75g/¼ tsp	*Lavang*/Cloves Powder
0.75g/¼ tsp	*Daalcheeni*/Cinnamon Powder
15ml/1 Tbs	Lemon Juice
2	Hard Boiled Eggs (quarter)
3.25g/1 Tbs	*Taaza Dhania*/Coriander (chop)

PREPARATION

THE CHICKEN: Carefully prise open the meat along the bone, pull the meat carefully to the opposite end, making sure that the bone does not get detached. Then flatten with a bat/steak hammer to make lollypop shaped escalopes.

THE MARINATION: Mix all the ingredients in a bowl, evenly rub the lollypops with this marinade and reserve for 1 hour.

COOKING

Melt enough *ghee* to cover a *lagan*/flat pan, place the marinated chicken escalopes, in the middle, and shallow-fry over very low heat, turning carefully once, until crisp and evenly golden (approx 10-12 minutes). Remove to absorbent paper to drain excess fat. Reserve the *ghee*

Melt 75g/6 Tbs of the reserved *ghee* (add more if there isn't enough left over) in a *handi*/pan, add garlic, saute over medium heat with a spatula until light golden, add onions and saute until onions become translucent and glossy. Add ginger and green chillies, and stir for a few seconds. Then add coriander, red chillies and turmeric powders (dissolved in 45ml.3 Tbs of water), *bhunno*/stir-fry until the moisture evaporates, add tomatoes and *bhunno*/stir-fry until they become soft and release their juices. Now add mince and salt, *bhunno*/stir-fry for 1ı-2 minutes, add chicken escalopes, stir carefully, add cardamom, clove and cinnamon powders, stir carefully, cover and cook on *dum* for 2 minutes. Remove and keep the *handi*/ pan covered for a few minutes. Uncover, add lemon juice, turn carefully with a spatula to incorporate, and adjust the seasoning.

TO SERVE

Remove to flat dish and garnish with eggs and coriander.

Khadhe Masaley ka Gosht

Serves: 4
Preparation time: 30 minutes
Cooking Time: 1 hour

INGREDIENTS

900 g	*Boti* of Kid/Lamb (1½" cubes)

The Gravy

125g	*Desi Ghee* (clarified butter)
5	*Chhotti Elaichi*/Green Cardamom
3	*Lavang*/Cloves
2	*Motti Elaichi*/Black Cardamom
2 sticks	*Daalcheeni*/Cinnamon (1")
2	Bay Leaves
12	Black Peppercorns
2g/1 tsp	*Dhania*/Coriander Seeds
30g/5¼ tsp	Garlic Paste (strained)
20g/3½ tsp	Ginger Paste (strained)
	Salt
250g/1 cup	Yoghurt
15g/1 Tbs	*Dhania*/Coriander Powder
3g/1 tsp	Red Chilli Powder
3g/1 tsp	*Haldee*/Turmeric Powder
60g/2 oz	Fried Onion Paste
30g/1 oz	Fried Garlic Paste
15g/½ oz	Cashewnut Paste
1 litre/4¼ cups	Clear Lamb Stock (or water)
1.5g/½ tsp	Green Cardamom Powder
0.75g/¼ tsp	Mace Powder
15ml/1 Tbs	Rosewater
1.6g/½ Tbs	*Dhania*/Coriander

PREPARATION

THE GRAVY: Put yoghurt in a bowl, add coriander, red chilli and turmeric powders, whisk and keep aside. Clean, wash and finely chop coriander.

COOKING

Heat *ghee* in a *handi*/pan, add green cardamom, cloves, black cardamom, cinnamon and bay leaves, peppercorns and coriander seeds, stir over medium heat until the cardamom begins to change colour, add the *boti*, *bhunno*/stir-fry to sear (approx 1½-2 minutes), add the garlic and ginger pastes and salt, *bhunno*/stir-fry until the liquid evaporates. Remove *handi*/pan from heat, stir-in the yoghurt mixture, return *handi*/pan to heat and *bhunno*/stir-fry until the fat leaves the sides. Then add the fried onion and garlic pastes, *bhunno*/stir-fry until the fat leaves the sides, add the cashewnut paste, *bhunno*/stir-fry until the fat leaves the sides, add the stock, bring to a boil, reduce to low heat and simmer, stirring occasionally, until the gravy is of thin sauce consistency. Add cardamom and mace powder, stir, add rose water, stir, remove and adjust the seasoning.

TO SERVE

Remove to a bowl, garnish with coriander and serve with *Chappati* or *Phulka*.

Khadhe Masaley ka Murg

Serves: 4

Preparation Time
45 minutes

Cooking Time
30 minutes

INGREDIENTS

800g/1 lb 13 oz	Chicken *Tikka* (2" cubes)
105g/½ cup	*Desi Ghee*/Clarified Butter
6	*Chhotti Elaichi*/Green Cardamom
3	*Lavang*/Cloves
2	*Tej Patta*/Bay Leaf
4g/2 tsp	*Jeera*/Cumin Seeds
4.5g/1½ tsp	Red Chilli Powder
3g/1 tsp	*Haldee*/Turmeric Powder
	Salt
25g/4 tsp	Ginger Paste (strain)
15g/2½ tsp	Garlic Paste (strain)
300g/11 oz	Onions (grate)
120g/4 oz	Yoghurt (whisk)
60g/2 oz	*Malaai*/Clotted Cream
6	Green Chillies (seed & halve lengthways)

COOKING

Heat *ghee* in a *handi*/pan, add green cardamom, cloves, bay leaves and cumin, stir over medium heat until the cumin begins to pop, add chicken, increase to high heat and sear for 1-1½ minutes. Reduce to medium heat, add red chillies, turmeric, salt, garlic and ginger, *bhunno*/stir-fry until specks of fat begin to appear on the surface. Then add 1 litre/4¼ cups of water and onions, bring to a boil, reduce to low heat, cover and simmer for 15 minutes. Uncover, stir-in yoghurt in a steady trickle, *bhunno*/stir-fry until specks of fat begin to appear on the surface. Now add green chillies, and *bhunno*/stir-fry until the onions are mashed. Remove and adjust the seasoning.

TO SERVE

Remove to a service dish, garnish with coriander, sprinkle pepper and serve with *Phulka*, *Khameeri Roti* or *Roomali Roti*.

Murg ki Chaamp

Serves: 4
Preparation Time 3:15 hours
Cooking Time 7-8 minutes

INGREDIENTS

12	Chicken Thighs
	Desi Ghee/Clarified Butter to cook

The Marination

30g/1 oz	Roasted Almond Paste
30g/1 oz	*Taaza Dhania*/Coriander Paste
30g/5 tsp	Ginger Paste (strain)
20g/3¼ tsp	Garlic Paste (strain)
10g/1¾ tsp	Green Chilli Paste
120g/½ cup	*Chakka Dahi*/Yoghurt Cheese/Hung Yoghurt
45ml/3 Tbs	Lemon Juice
45g/1½ oz	Fried Onion Paste
45g/1½ oz	Flour of Roasted *Channa* (Gram)
10g/1½ Tbs	*Kopra*/Desiccated Coconut
3g/1 tsp	Black Pepper (freshly roasted & coarsely ground)
1.5g/½ tsp	*Chhotti Elaichi*/Green Cardamom Powder
0.75/¼ tsp	*Lavang*/Clove Powder
0.75/¼ tsp	*Daalcheeni*/Cinnamon Powder
0.75/¼ tsp	*Javitri*/Mace Powder
0.75/¼ tsp	Kebab Cheeni Powder
	Salt
1g/2 tsp	*Zaafraan*/Saffron

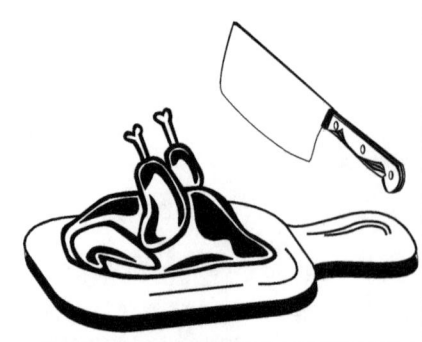

PREPARATION

THE CHICKEN: Carefully prise open the meat along the bone, pull the meat carefully to the opposite end, making sure that the bone does not get detached. Then flatten gently with a bat to make lollypops.

THE SAFFRON: Crush saffron threads with a pestle or the back of a spoon, reserve in 30ml/2 Tbs of lukewarm water for 20 minutes, and then make a paste.

THE MARINATION: Mix all the ingredients in a bowl, evenly rub the lollypops with this marinade and reserve for 1 hour.

COOKING

Spread enough *ghee* to cover a *lagan*/flat pan, place the marinated chicken, including the marinade, in the middle, and cook over very low heat, turning carefully once, until crisp and evenly golden (approx 7-8 minutes). Remove to absorbent paper to drain excess fat.

TO SERVE

Remove to flat dish and serve with spring onions and tomatoes.

NOTE: All weights are nett, i.e., post PREPARATION, and not gross.

Maas ki Kadhi

Serves: 4

Preparation Time
35 minutes

Cooking Time
2.15 hours

INGREDIENTS

1kg/2¼ lb	Leg of Spring Lamb

The Marination
100g/½ cup	Ghee
5g/1¾ tsp	*Jeera*/Cumin seeds
	A generous pinch Asafoetida
100g/½ cup	Boiled Onion paste
50g/3 Tbs	Garlic paste
400g/1¾ cup	Yoghurt (1-day old)
50g/⅓ cup	Gramflour
5g/1 tsp	Red Chilli powder
3g/½ tsp	*Haldee*/Turmeric
	Salt
8	Green Chillies
20g/⅓ cup	*Dhania*/Coriander

PREPARATION

THE LAMB: Clean, debone and cut into 1-inch *boti*.
THE CUMIN: Broil half the seeds on a *tawa*, cool, put in a grinder and make a powder.
THE YOGHURT: Whisk yoghurt in a bowl, add gramflour, red chillies, turmeric and salt, mix well. Add water (approx 800 ml/ 3⅓ cup) and whisk again
THE VEGETABLES: Remove stems, wash, slit, deseed and finely chop green chillies. Clean, wash and chop coriander.

COOKING

Heat ghee in a *kadhai*, add cumin seeds and asafoetida, sauté over medium heat until the seeds begin to crackle. Add the lamb chunks and salt, *bhunno* until evenly light brown, add the boiled onion and garlic pastes, *bhunno* for 3-4 minutes. Then add water (approx 600ml/2½ cups), bring to a boil, cover and simmer, stirring occasionally, until meat is almost tender. Now add the yoghurt mixture, bring to a boil, reduce to medium heat and cook, stirring constantly, until the gravy starts getting thick (approx 8-10 minutes). Add cumin powder and green chillies, stir and cook for 2-3 minutes. Adjust the seasoning.

TO SERVE

Remove to a bowl, garnish with coriander and serve with boiled rice.

Note: Buttermilk (1.2 litres/5 cups) is better suited for *Kadhi* than a mixture of yoghurt and water.

Akhaa Aad Dhungaar

Serves: 4
Preparation Time 4:30 hours
Cooking Time up to 30 minutes

INGREDIENTS

2	Duck (make deep incision—3 on each breast, 2 on each thigh, 3 on each drumstick) *Desi Ghee*/Clarified Butter for basting

The First Marination

90ml/6 Tbs	Vinegar
60g/2 oz	Raw Papaya Paste
20g/3½ tsp	Garlic Paste (strain)
10g/1¾ tsp	Ginger Paste (strain)
6g/2 tsp	Red Chilli Powder
60ml/¼ cup	Cooking Oil
	Salt

The Second Marination

200g/7 oz	*Chakka Dahi*/Yoghurt Cheese (whisk)
20g/3½ tsp	Garlic Paste (strain)
10g/1¾ tsp	Ginger Paste (strain)
3g/1tsp	Red Chilli Powder
3g/1 tsp	Black Pepper Powder (coarsely ground)
1.5g/½ tsp	*Jeera*/Cumin Powder
1.5g/½ tsp	*Daalcheeni*/Cinnamon Powder
0.75g/¼ tsp	*Motti Elaichi*/Black Cardamom Powder
0.75g/¼ tsp	*Lavang*/Clove Powder
0.75g/¼ tsp	*Jaiphal*/Nutmeg Powder
	A generous pinch *Kaala Namak*/Black Rock Salt Powder
	Salt

The Smoking

4	*Chhotti Elaichi*/Green Cardamom
12.5g/1 Tbs	*Desi Ghee*/Clarified Butter

PREPARATION

THE FIRST MARINATION: Put all the ingredients in a tray and mix well. Evenly rub the ducks with this marinade and reserve for 3 hours.

THE SECOND MARINATION: Put all the ingredients in a bowl and mix well. Evenly rub the ducks with the second marinade and reserve in the refrigerator for 1 hour.

THE SMOKING: Place the ducks alongside each other in a large *handi*/pan. Put a few small places of 'live' charcoal in small *katori*/metal bowl in between the two ducks.

Crush the green cardamom, put on the charcoal, let it begin to change colour, pour on ghee, cover with a lid and let it smoke for 30 minutes. Uncover, remove the *katori*/metal bowl and discard.

THE OVEN: Pre-heat to 350°F.

THE SKEWERING: Skewer the ducks, without any gaps, and keep a tray underneath to collect the drippings

COOKING

Roast in a moderately hot tandoor/on charcoal grill for 12-15 minutes. Remove and hang the skewers to allow the excess moisture to drip off (approx. 3-4 minutes), baste and roast again for 3-4 minutes. In the pre-heated oven, roast the ducks for 30 minutes, basting at regular intervals.

Akhaa Peenda

Serves: 8
Preparation Time 1:30 hours
Cooking Time 2:30 hours
Finishing Time 5-7 minutes

INGREDIENTS

2	Leg of Kid/Lamb (1.2 Kg/2¼ lb each)
	Sarson/Mustard Oil to rub (optional)
	Cooking Oil to taste
	Unsalted Butter to brush

The Studding
12	*Lavang*/Cloves
12 flakes	Garlic
4 sticks	*Daalcheeni*/Cinnamon (1")
24	Black Peppercorns

The Marination
9g/1 Tbs	Red Chilli Powder
	Salt
90ml/6 Tbs	Rum
60ml/¼ cup	Malt Vinegar
50g/3 Tbs	Ginger Paste (strain)
20g/3½ tsp	Garlic Paste (strain)

The Braising
5	*Chhotti Elaichi*/Green Cardamom
2	*Motti Elaichi*/Black Cardamom
4 sticks	*Daalcheeni*/Cinnamon (1")
2	*Tej Patta*/Bay Leaf
12	Black Peppercorns
2.5g/1 tsp	*Shahi Jeera*/Black Cumin Seeds
30ml/2 Tbs	Mustard Oil

The *Raan Masala*
15g/5 tsp	*Amchoor*
4.5g/1½ tsp	*Kasoori Methi* Powder
3g/1 tsp	Black Pepper Powder
1.5g/½ tsp	Black Cardamom Powder
1.5g/½ tsp	Black Rock Salt

PREPARATION

THE KID/LAMB LEGS: Clean, prick with a fork, wash and pat dry.

THE STUDDING: Using a cooking needle, stud the legs with equal numbers of cloves, flakes of garlic, cinnamon and peppercorns. Reserve for 30 minutes.

THE MARINATION: Mix salt with red chillies and vigorously massage the legs with this mixture. Mix the remaining ingredients, evenly rub the legs with this marinade and reserve for an hour.

THE OVEN: Pre-heat to 350°F.

THE BRAISING: Put the legs in a roasting tray, spread the spices and mustard oil on and around the legs, add enough water to cover the legs, cover with silver foil, puncture two holes in the foil and braise in a pre-heated oven for an hour. Reduce oven temperature to 275°F and continue to braise until meat is tender and leaves bones from the ends (approx 2-2½ hours). Remove, evenly rub with mustard oil and allow the legs to cool.

THE *RAAN MASALA*: Mix all the ingredients and store in a sterilised glass jar.

THE SKEWERING: Skewer right down middle horizontally and as close to bone as possible.

FINISHING

Roast in moderately hot tandoor for 6-7 minutes, remove, baste with cooking oil and roast again for 2 minutes. Or, arrange leg on mesh of charcoal grill, cover grill and roast over moderate heat for 7-8 minutes. Uncover, baste with cooking oil and roast again for 2 minutes. Alternatively, arrange leg on greased roasting tray and put in pre-heated (350°F) oven for 7-8 minutes. Baste with oil and roast again for 3 minutes. Remove.

TO SERVE

Baste leg with butter, arrange on carving platter, sprinkle a generous pinch or two of the *Raan Masala* and serve.

Laal Maas

Serves: 4
Preparation Time 30 minutes
Cooking Time 1:45 hours

INGREDIENTS

1 Kg/2¼ lb	Shoulder of Kid/Lamb (1½" *boti*/cubes)
30	Whole Dried Red Chillies (wipe, slit, seed & discard stems)
150g/5 oz	*Desi Ghee*/Clarified Butter
60g/2 oz	Garlic (slice)
200g/1½ cup	Onions (finely slice)
5	*Chhotti Elaichi*/Green Cardamom
3	*Motti Elaichi*/Black Cardamom
2g/1 tsp	*Jeera*/Cumin Seeds (broil/roast on a *tawa*/griddle)
260g/1 cup	Yoghurt
15g/5 tsp	*Dhania*/Coriander Powder
3g/1 tsp	*Haldee*/Turmeric Powder
	Salt

PREPARATION

THE YOGHURT: Put in a bowl, add cumin, coriander powder, turmeric and salt, whisk to mix well and keep aside for 10 minutes.

COOKING

Heat *ghee* in a *handi*/pan, add garlic and *bhunno*/stir-fry over medium heat until light golden, add red chillies, onions, black cardamom and green cardamom and cumin seeds, *bhunno*/stir-fry until onions are golden brown. Then add meat, increase to high heat, *bhunno*/stir-fry to sear for 3-4 minutes or until the meat changes colour, reduce to medium heat, cover and simmer, stirring occasionally, for 10 minutes. Uncover and *bhunno*/stir-fry until fat leaves the sides. Remove *handi*/pan, stir-in the yoghurt mixture, return *handi*/pan to heat and *bhunno*/stir-fry until fat leaves the sides. Now add water (approx 1.4 litres/6 cups), bring to a boil, reduce to low heat, cover and simmer, stirring occasionally, until the meat is cooked and the gravy is of thin sauce consistency (approx 25 minutes). Remove and adjust the seasoning.

Note: All weights are nett, i.e., post PREPARATION, and not gross.

THE REGAL REPAST

Maalgoba

Serves: 4

Preparation Time
30 minutes

Cooking Time
1 hour

INGREDIENTS

900g/2 lb	Kid/Spring Lamb Shoulder (1½" cubes)
150g/¾ cup	*Desi Ghee*/Clarified Butter
120g/4 oz	Onions (finely slice)
3	*Motti Elaichi*/Black Cardamom
4	*Lavang*/Cloves
8	Black Peppercorns
9g/1 Tbs	*Maida*/All-purpose Flour
6.5g/2 Tbs	*Taaza Dhania*/Coriander (chop)
	Salt
9g/1 Tbs	*Dhania*/Coriander Powder
3g/1 tsp	*Haldee*/Turmeric Powder
6g/2 tsp	Red Chilli Powder
20g/2" piece	Ginger Paste (mince)
1 litre/4 cups	Yoghurt

PREPARATION

THE YOGHURT: Put in a bowl, add flour and whisk to mix well. (The yoghurt should be absolutely fresh, as it provides the main flavour.)

COOKING

Heat *ghee*/clarified butter in a *handi*/pan, add cardamom, cloves and pepper, stir over medium heat for a few seconds, add onions and *bhunno*/stir-fry until onions are golden brown. Then add meat, salt, coriander and turmeric, and *bhunno*/stir-fry for 4-5 minutes, adding small quantities of water at regular intervals. Add red chillies and ginger, *bhunno*/stir-fry for 3-4 minutes, adding small quantities of water at regular intervals. Now add approx 1 litre/4¼ cups of water, bring to a boil, reduce to low heat, cover and simmer, stirring occasionally, until meat is cooked and the liquid evaporates. Remove *handi*/pan from heat, stir-in the yoghurt mixture, return *handi*/pan to heat, add coriander, stir, cover and cook on *dum* until fat comes to the surface. Remove, uncover and adjust the seasoning.

TO SERVE

Remove to a service bowl, garnish with coriander and serve with *Chappati*, *Tandoori Roti* or steamed rice.

Maas ke Sooley

Serves: 4
Preparation Time 4:30 hours
Cooking Time 10 minutes/batch

INGREDIENTS

24	Piccata of Kid/Lamb (3" x 2" x ¼"; from the *Dasti*/Shoulder) *Desi Ghee*/Clarified Butter to baste

The Marination

60g/¼ cup	*Chakka Dahi*/Yoghurt Cheese/Hung Yoghurt
45g/1½ oz	Fried Onion Paste
45g/3 Tbs	*Kachri* Powder
30g/1 oz	Roasted Almond Paste
30g/5 tsp	Garlic Paste (strain)
20g/3½ tsp	Ginger Paste (strain)
6g/2 tsp	Red Chilli Powder
37.5g/3 Tbs	*Desi Ghee*/Clarified Butter
4.5g/1½ tsp	*Kaali Mirch*/Black Pepper (fresh roasted & coarsely ground)
4.5g/1½ tsp	*Dhania*/Coriander Powder
4.5g/1½ tsp	*Amchoor*/Mango Powder
1.5g/½ tsp	*Lavang*/Clove Powder
1.5g/½ tsp	*Motti Elaichi*/Black Cardamom Powder
0.75g/¼ tsp	*Chhotti Elaichi*/Green Cardamom Powder
0.75g/¼ tsp	*Daalcheeni*/Cinnamon Powder
0.375g/⅛ tsp	*Javitri*/Mace Powder
0.375g/⅛ tsp	*Jaiphal*/Nutmeg Powder
	A generous pinch of *Kaala Namak*/Black Rock Salt
15ml/1 Tbs	Lemon Juice
	Salt

The Smoking

5	Cloves
4.5g/1 tsp	*Desi Ghee*/Clarified Butter

PREPARATION

THE MARINATION: Mix all the ingredients in a bowl, evenly rub the picatta with this marinade and keep aside.

THE SMOKING: Put a few small pieces of 'live' charcoal in a small *katori*/metal bowl and place the *katori*/metal bowl in a large *handi*/pan. Spread the *sooley* around the *katori*/metal bowl, place cloves on the charcoal, pour on the *ghee* and, as the smoke begins to billow, cover with a lid and reserve for 4 hours.

THE SKEWERING: Uncover, remove the *katori*/metal bowl, carefully skewer *sooley* in convenient batches, penetrating the meat twice, on thin skewers and the spread to ensure minimum curling.

COOKING

Roast on a moderately hot charcoal grill for 8-10 minutes, basting with *ghee* at regular intervals.

TO SERVE

Unskewer, arrange *sooley* on platter, sprinkle the reserved *Special Masala* and serve with onion rings and lemon wedges.

Gol Maas Kaacher

Serves: 4
Preparation Time 45 minutes
Cooking Time 1:30 hours

INGREDIENTS

1.2 kg/2¼ lb	Leg of Kid/Lamb
250g/11 oz	Fresh *Kachri*
90ml/6 Tbs	Mustard Oil
250g/9 oz	Onions
30g/5 tsp	Garlic Paste (strain)
15g/2½ tsp	Ginger Paste (strain)
5	*Chhotti Elaichi*/Green Cardamom
2	*Lavang*/Cloves
1 stick	*Daalcheeni*/Cinnamon (1")
1	*Tej Patta*/Bay Leaf
90ml/3 oz	Yoghurt
150ml/5 oz	Tomato Purée
4.5g/1½ tsp	Red Chilli Powder
	Salt
0.75g/¼ tsp	*Chhotti Elaichi*/Green Cardamom Powder
0.75g/¼ tsp	*Motti Elaichi*/Black Cardamom Powder
0.375g/⅛ tsp	*Jaiphal*/Nutmeg Powder
0.375g/⅛ tsp	*Lavang*/Clove Powder
0.375g/⅛ tsp	*Daalcheeni*/Cinnamon Powder

The Garnish

4	Green Chillies
2	Lemons

PREPARATION

THE MUTTON: Clean, bone, cut into 1" cubes, wash and pat dry.
THE *KACHRI*: Scrape, wash and slice into roundels.
THE ONIONS: Peel, wash and slice onions. Reserve 100g/3 oz, transfer the remaining onions to a blender and make a purée.
THE YOGHURT MIXTURE: Put yoghurt in a bowl, add tomato purée, red chilli powder and salt, whisk and keep aside.
THE GARNISH: Wash green chillies, slit, seed, remove the stem and cut into juliennes. Wash and cut the lemon into wedges.

COOKING

Heat mustard oil to a smoking point in a *kadhai*/wok, remove and sprinkle a little water (to bring the temperature down quickly, though this must be done carefully or the splattering may cause burns; alternatively, remove and cool until moderately hot.) Reheat, add the sliced onions, *bhunno*/stir-fry over medium heat until light brown, add the garlic and ginger pastes, and *bhunno*/stir-fry until the moisture evaporates. Then add green cardamom, cloves, cinnamon and bay leaf, stir, add onion purée, stir, add the meat and *bhunno*/stir-fry until the fat leaves the masala. Remove *handi*/pan from heat, stir-in the yoghurt mixture, return *handi*/pan to heat, bring to a boil, reduce to low heat, cover and simmer, stirring occasionally, until the meat is almost cooked. Now add the *kachri* roundels, stir, increase to medium heat and cook until the meat is cooked, the *kachri* is tender, and both are napped (approx 7-8 minutes). Sprinkle green cardamom powder, black cardamom powder, nutmeg powder, clove powder, and cinnamon powder, stir, remove and adjust the seasoning.

TO SERVE

Remove to a bowl, garnish with green chilli juliennes and lemon wedges and serve with *Phulka*.

Note: All weights are nett, i.e. post PREPARATION, and not gross.

Safaed Maas

Serves: 4
Preparation Time: 1:45 hours
Cooking Time: 1 hour

INGREDIENTS

12 Kid/Lamb Shanks (*Kareli/Nalli*)

The Marination
60g/2 oz	Yoghurt Cheese/Hung Yoghurt/*Chakka Dahi*
30g/5 tsp	Garlic Paste
15g/2½ tsp	Ginger Paste
5g/¾ tsp	Green Chilli Paste
3g/1 tsp	Coriander Powder
1.5g/½ tsp	White Pepper Powder
	Salt

The Gravy
70g/6 Tbs	*Desi Ghee*
4	*Chhotti Eliachi*/Green Cardamaom
3	*Lavang*/Cloves
	Salt
2	*Tej Patta*/Bay Leaf
3 blades	Mace
2g/1 tsp	*Sabut Dhania*/Coriander Seeds
100g/3 oz	Onions
200g/7 oz	Boiled Onion Paste
20g/3¾ tsp	Almond Paste
10g/1½ tsp	Melon Seed Paste
30g/1 oz	Coconut
150g	*Dahi*/Yoghurt
6g/2 tsp	*Dhania*/Coriander Powder
720ml/3 cups	Lamb Stock
3g/1 tsp	Black Pepper Powder (freshly and coarsely ground)
2.25g/¾ tsp	Green Cardamom Powder
0.75g/¼ tsp	Mace Powder
60ml/¼ cup	Cream
5ml/1 tsp	*Gulaabjal* (Rose Water)
15ml/1 Tbs	Lemon Juice

PREPARATION

THE MEAT: Clean the *nalli* (shanks), remove the sinews, wash and pat dry. (Ask the butcher for *nalli* or shanks, ensuring they are open-ended on both sides.) Then remove the meat by carefully scraping along the length of the shanks starting at narrower end, to expose the bone, leaving an inch from the other end. (This is done so that when the meat is braised, it shrivels at the unexposed end, making the shank easy to cut at the time of eating. Also, it makes the dish more attractive). Reserve the bones for the stock.

THE MARINATION: Put yoghurt cheese in a bowl, add the remaining ingredients, whisk to mix well, evenly rub the meat with this marinade and reserve for at least an hour.

THE GRAVY: Soak coriander seeds in water overnight and drain at the time of use. Peel, wash and chop onions. Remove the brown skin and grate coconut. (Of course, there's nothing that can match the *malaai* of what most people call 'tender coconut'.) Mix with the almond and melon seed pastes. Put yoghurt in a bowl, add coriander powder and salt, whisk to mix well.

COOKING

Heat *desi ghee* in a *handi*/pan, add green cardamom, cloves, bay leaves, mace and the soaked coriander seeds, stir over medium heat until the green cardamom changes colour, add the garlic and ginger pastes (dissolved in 30ml/2 Tbs of water), *bhunno*/stir-fry until the moisture evaporates, ensuring that the masala does not get coloured. Add the marinated meat, increase to high heat, and *bhunno*/stir-fry to sear and seal-in the juices (approx 4-5 minutes). Then add the chopped onions, *bhunno*/stir-fry until translucent and glossy, add the boiled onion paste, *bhunno*/stir-fry until specks of fat begin to appear on the surface (ensuring that the masala should not get coloured), add the almond paste-melon seed paste-coconut mixture, *bhunno*/stir-fry until specks of fat begin to appear on the surface (ensuring that the masala should not be coloured). Remove *handi*/pan from heat, stir-in the yoghurt mixture, return *handi*/pan to heat, *bhunno*/stir-fry until the fat leaves the sides (ensuring that the masala does not get coloured), add stock, bring to a boil, reduce to low heat, cover and simmer, stirring occasionally and carefully, until the meat is cooked (add more stock, if necessary). Reduce to low heat, simmer until of thin sauce consistency, add black pepper, cardamom and mace powders, stir. Remove, stir-in cream, add rose water and lemon juice, stir and adjust the seasoning.

TO SERVE

Arrange 3 shanks on each of 4 individual plates, pour equal quantities of the gravy and serve with *Roti* or *Phulka*.

Mewar ka Khaas Maas

Serves: 4

Preparation Time
45 minutes

Cooking Time
1:15 hours

INGREDIENTS

600g/1lb 5 oz	Leg of Kid/Lamb
8	Kid/Lamb Chops (single rib)
75g/5 Tbs	*Desi Ghee*/Clarified Butter
300g/11 oz	Onions
	Salt
1 litre/4¼ cups	Clear Kid/Lamb Stock
10g/1¼ tsp	Garlic Paste (strain)
10g/1¼ tsp	Ginger Paste (strain)
8	*Chhotti Elaichi*/Green Cardamom
5	*Lavang*/Cloves
2 sticks	*Daalcheeni*/Cinnamon (1")
4.5g/1¼ tsp	*Dhania*/Coriander Powder
3g/1 tsp	Red Chilli Powder
2.25g/¾ tsp	*Haldee*/Turmeric Powder
150g/5 oz	Yoghurt
10g/4 tsp	*Besan*/Gramflour
10ml/2 tsp	Cooking Oil
15g/1 Tbs	Cashewnut Paste
½	*Jaiphal*/Nutmeg
2 drops	Kewra
6.5g/2 Tbs	*Taaza Dhania*/Coriander
2	Green Chillies

PREPARATION

THE KID/LAMB: Clean, bone, wash, pat dry and cut into 1" chunks.

THE CHOPS: Clean, trim, wash and pat dry.

THE VEGETABLES: Peel, wash and slice onions. Clean, wash and chop coriander. Wash green chillies, halve, seed and discard the stems.

THE YOGHURT: Whisk in a bowl.

THE *BESAN*: Heat oil in a *kadhai*/wok, add the gramflour and *bhunno*/stir-fry over medium heat until it emits its unique aroma.

THE NUTMEG: Grate in a bowl.

COOKING

Heat *ghee* in a *handi*/pan, add half the onions, sauté over medium heat until light golden, add the meat, and *bhunno*/stir-fry over high heat to sear for 2-3 minutes. Add the remaining onions, salt and 120ml/2 cup of stock, stir, add the garlic and ginger pastes, and stir. Then add green cardamom, cloves and cinnamon, stir, add the coriander, red chilli and turmeric powders, and *bhunno*/stir-fry until the fat leaves the sides. Remove *handi*/pan from heat, stir-in yoghurt, return *handi*/pan to heat and *bhunno*/stir-fry until the liquid evaporates. Add 120ml/2 cup of stock and *bhunno*/stir-fry until the liquid evaporates. Repeat the process twice more. Now add the cooked gramflour, stir until fully incorporated, add cashew nut paste, stir until fully incorporated, add nutmeg, stir, add the remaining stock, bring to a boil, add *kewra* and remove. Cover the *handi*/pan with a lid, seal with *atta* dough, return *handi*/pan to heat and cook on *dum* (over very low heat) for 30 minutes. Remove *handi*/pan from heat, break the seal, uncover and adjust the seasoning

TO SERVE

Remove to a service dish, garnish with coriander and green chillies, and serve with *Roomali Roti* or *Phulka*.

Adlah

Serves: 4
Preparation Time 45 minutes
Cooking Time 1:30 hours

INGREDIENTS

12	*Nalli*/Shanks of Kid/Lamb (3½" long bone)
6	*Chhotti Elaichi*/Green Cardamom
4	*Lavang*/Cloves
2	*Tej Patta*/Bay Leaf
2g/1 tsp	*Jeera*/Cumin Seeds
350g/13 oz	Onions (slice)
3g/1 tsp	*Haldee*/Turmeric Powder
	Salt
30g/5¼ tsp	Garlic Paste (strain)
20g/3½ tsp	Ginger Paste (strain)
60g/2 oz	*Malaai*/Clotted Cream
150g/5 oz	Yoghurt (whisk)
75g/6 Tbs	*Desi Ghee*/Clarified Butter
1.5g/½ tsp	*Chhotti Elaichi*/Green Cardamom Powder
0.75g/¼ tsp	*Javitri*/Mace Powder
0.375g/⅛ tsp	*Jaiphal*/Nutmeg Powder
0.375g/⅛ tsp	*Daalcheeni*/Cinnamon Powder
0.375g/⅛ tsp	*Lavang*/Clove Powder

COOKING

Put shanks in a *handi*/pan, add cardamom, cloves, bay leaves, cumin, onions, turmeric, red chilli powder, salt and 720ml/3 cups of water, bring to a boil, reduce to low heat, cover and simmer for 7-8 minutes. Uncover, add garlic and ginger, cover and simmer for 10 minutes. Uncover, add clotted cream, cover and simmer for 15 minutes. Uncover, add yoghurt, cover and simmer for 20 minutes. Uncover, add *ghee* and *bhunno*/stir-fry until the onions are completely mashed but not coloured. Then add 720ml/3 cups of water, bring to a boil, reduce to low heat, and simmer until the meat is cooked (approx 10 minutes) and the gravy is of thin sauce, but grainy (on account of the onions) consistency. Sprinkle the powdered spices, stir, remove and adjust the seasoning.

TO SERVE

Remove to a service dish and serve with *Roomali Roti*.

Makki ka Soweta

Serves: 4
Preparation Time
1.30 hours
Cooking Time
1.30 hours

INGREDIENTS

750g/½ lb	Spring Lamb (assorted cuts)
450g/1 lb	Corn on the Cob
150g/¾ cup	*Ghee*/Clarified Butter
3g/1 tsp	*Jeera*/Cumin Seeds
4	*Chhotti Elaichi*/Green Cardamom
4	*Motti Elaichi*/Black Cardamom
8	*Lavang*/Cloves
2 sticks	*Dalcheeni*/Cinnamon (1-inch)
2	*Tej Patta*/Bay Leaf
300 ml/1¼ cup	Milk
30ml/2 Tbs	Lemon juice
20g/⅓ cup	*Sabut Dhania*/Coriander

The Paste

160g/1 cup	Onions
50g/5 Tbs	Garlic
8	Green Chillies

The Marination

225g/1 cup	Yoghurt
10g/2 tsp	*Dhania*/Coriander powder
5g/1 tsp	Red Chilli powder
3g/½ tsp	*Haldee*/Turmeric
	Salt

PREPARATION

THE LAMB: Clean and cut breast and saddle into 12-inch chunks. Clean chops.

THE CORN: Boil, cool and grate the kernels on the cob. (If using canned corn, roughly chop.)

THE PASTE: Peel, wash and roughly cut onions. Peel garlic. Remove stems, wash, slit and deseed green chillies. Put these ingredients in a blender and make a fine paste.

THE MARINATION: Whisk yoghurt in a large bowl, add the paste, coriander powder, red chillies, turmeric and salt, mix well. Leave the meat in this marinade for at least 45 minutes.

THE CORIANDER: Clean, wash and chop.

COOKING

Heat ghee in a *handi*, add cumin seeds, the cardamom, cloves, cinnamon and bay leaves, sauté over medium heat until the seeds begin to crakle. Add the lamb chunks, along with marinade, and *bhunno* until evenly brown and the moisture has evaporated. Add water (approx 750ml/3 cups), bring to a boil, cover and simmer until meat is almost cooked. Now add the grated corn and milk, cook, stirring constantly, for 8-10 minutes. Remove, add lemon juice and stir. Adjust the seasoning.

TO SERVE

Remove to a shallow dish, garnish with coriander and serve as a meal.

Bharwaan Pasandey

Serves: 4
Preparation Time: 1.30 hours
Cooking Time: 30 minutes

INGREDIENTS

16	*Pasanda*/Piccatta of Kid/Lamb (45g/1½ oz each)
	Desi Ghee/Clarified Butter to braise *pasanda*

The Marination

15g/2½ tsp	Garlic Paste (strain)
15g/2½ tsp	Ginger Paste (strain)
4.5/1½ tsp	*Kachri* Powder
2.25g/¾ tsp	Red Chilli Powder
	Salt

The Filling

150g/5 oz	Onions (finely chop)
60g/2 oz	*Chakka Dahi*/Yoghurt Cheese/Hung Yoghurt
30g/1 oz	Processed/Cheddar Cheese (grate)
17.5g/½ cup	*Taaza Pudhina*/Mint (finely chop)
6g/1 tsp	Green Chilli Paste
1.5g/½ tsp	*Chotti Elaichi*/Green Cardamom Powder
24	Pistachio (crush to a fine powder)

The Gravy

105g/½ cup	*Desi Ghee*/Clarified Butter
6	*Lavang*/Cloves
5	*Chotti Elaichi*/Green Cardamon
4	*Motti Elaichi*/Black Cardamom
2	*Daalcheeni*/Cinnamon (1")
1	*Tej Patta*/Bay Leaf
8	Whole Red Chillies (break into 1" pieces & seed)
12	Peppercorns
15g/2½ tsp	Ginger Paste (strain)
15g/2½ tsp	Garlic Paste (strain)
300g/11 oz	Onions (grate)
120g/4 oz	Yoghurt
12g/4 tsp	*Dhania*/Coriander Powder
	Salt

PREPARATION

THE *PASANDA*: Clean, trim, wash, pat dry and flatten with a bat into ⅛" thick picatta.

THE MARINATION: Mix all the ingredients in a large bowl, evenly rub the *pasanda* with this marinade and reserve for 45 minutes.

THE FILLING: Mix all the ingredients in a bowl and divide into 16 equal portions.

THE STUFFING: Place a portion of the filling in each *pasanda*, roll and secure with a toothpick.

THE BRAISING: Heat *ghee* in a large frying pan, arrange the *pasanda* in it and braise over high heat until evenly seared. Remove to absorbent paper to drain excess fat and then remove the toothpicks. Reserve the *ghee*.

THE YOGHURT MIXTURE: Put yoghurt in a bowl, add coriander powder and salt, and whisk to mix well.

COOKING

Reheat the reserved *ghee* (add additional *ghee* if necessary—you'll need 105g/½ cup) in a *handi*/pan, add cloves, green cardamom, black cardamom, , cinnamon and bay leaf, stir until green cardamom begins to change colour, add pepper and red chillies, stir over medium heat until the chillies begin to change colour. Then add the ginger and garlic, *bhunno*/stir-fry until specks of fat begin to appear on the surface. Then add 1-litre/4¼ cups of water and onions, bring to a boil, reduce to low heat, cover and simmer for 15 minutes. Uncover, stir-in yoghurt in a steady trickle, *bhunno*/stir-fry until the onions are mashed, add *pasanda* and cook for 4-5 minutes or until cooked. Remove and adjust the seasoning.

Chaamp Badaami

Serves: 4
Preparation Time: 3.30 hours
Cooking Time: 1 hour

INGREDIENTS

12	Kid/Lamb Chops (3-bone)
60g/5 Tbs	Unsalted Butter

The Marination

60ml/¼ cup	*Sirka*/Malt Vinegar
120g/½ cup	Yoghurt
30g/5 tsp	Garlic Paste (strain)
20g/3½ tsp	Ginger Paste (strain)
20g/1 Tbs	Fried Onion Paste
15g/2½ tsp	Raw Papaya Paste
1.5g/½ tsp	Red Chilli Powder
1.5g/½ tsp	*Chhotti Elaichi*/Green Cardamom Powder
0.75g/¼ tsp	*Lavang*/Clove Powder
	A pinch *Jaiphal*/Nutmeg Powder
	Salt

The Gravy

75g/6 Tbs	*Desi Ghee*/Clarified Butter
5	*Chhotti Elaichi*/Green Cardamon
3	*Lavang*/Cloves
2 sticks	*Daalcheeni*/Cinnamon (1")
2	*Tej Patta*/Bay Leaf
30g/5 tsp	Garlic Paste (strain)
20g/3½ tsp	Ginger Paste (strain)
75g/2½ oz	Almonds
	Desi Ghee/Clarified Butter to deep-fry almonds
60g/3 Tbs	Fried Onion Paste
30g/1½ Tbs	Fried Garlic Paste
3g/1 tsp	Red Chilli Powder
	Salt
0.75g/¼ tsp	*Chhotti Elaichi*/Green Cardamom Powder
0.75g/¼ tsp	*Lavang*/Clove Powder
0.75g/¼ tsp	*Daalcheeni*/Cinnamon Powder
0.375g/⅛ tsp	*Javitri*/Mace Powder
0.375g/⅛ tsp	*Jaiphal*/Nutmeg Powder
1 drop	Ittar

The Garnish

4	Almonds
0.25g/½ tsp	*Zaafraan*/Saffron

PREPARATION

THE CHOPS: Clean, trim, remove the two side ribs and then carefully scrape off the meat from the lower part of the bones.

THE MARINATION: Whisk yoghurt in a large bowl, add the remaining ingredients, rub the chops with this marinade and reserve for at least 3 hours.

THE GRAVY: Blanch almonds in boiling water, drain, cool and peel. Heat *ghee* in a *kadhai*/wok, add the almonds and deep fry over medium heat until light golden. Remove to absorbent paper to drain excess fat and cool, put in a blender, add water (approx 60ml/1 cup) and make a smooth paste. Remove and keep aside.

THE GARNISH: Blanch almonds in boiling water, drain, cool, peel and cut into slivers. Crush saffron threads with a pestle or the back of a spoon, soak in lukewarm water, make a paste and then soak the slivers in the saffron.

THE OVEN: Pre-heat to 275°F.

COOKING

Arrange the chops in a greased roasting tray, spread the marinade evenly on the chops, put knobs of butter on top and bake in the pre-heated oven until cooked, basting at regular intervals with the marinade (approx 25 minutes). Remove the chops and reserve the liquor.

Heat *ghee* in a *handi*/pan, add cardamom, cloves, cinnamon and bay leaves, and stir over medium heat until the cardamom begins to change colour. Add the garlic and ginger pastes, *bhunno*/stir-fry until the moisture evaporates, reduce to low heat, add the almond paste and *bhunno*/stir-fry until brown, adding small quantities of water at regular intervals to ensure that the *masala* does not burn and acquire a bitter taste. Increase to medium heat, add the fried onion and garlic pastes, *bhunno*/stir-fry until the fat leaves the sides, add red chillies, stir for 30 seconds, add the reserved liquor and *bhunno*/stir-fry until the fat leaves the sides. Then add water (approx 480ml/2 cups), bring to a boil, reduce to low heat and simmer for 4-5 minutes. Remove and pass the gravy through a fine-mesh soup strainer into a separate *handi*/pan, return gravy to heat, add salt, cardamom, clove, cinnamon, mace and nutmeg powders, stir, bring to a boil, reduce to low heat, add the chops and simmer, stirring occasionally, until the chops are napped. Remove, add *ittar*, stir and adjust the seasoning.

TO SERVE

Glaze the chops under the top heat of the pre-heated oven until coloured, arrange 3 on each of 4 individual plates, garnish with almonds and serve with *Phulka, Tawa Paratha* or *Sheermal*.

Gobhi Rajwadi

Serves: 4
Preparation Time
45 minutes
Cooking Time
8-10 minutes

INGREDIENTS

600g/1lb 5 oz	Cauliflower (medium florets)
250g/9 oz	*Zimikand/Sooran*/Yam (½" cubes; boil until soft)
65g/5 Tbs	*Desi Ghee*/Clarified Butter
2g/1 tsp	*Jeera*/Cumin Seeds
90g/3 oz	Onions (chop)
6 flakes	Garlic (chop)
15g/1½" piece	Ginger (chop)
6g/2 tsp	*Kachri* Powder
6g/2 tsp	*Dhania*/Coriander Powder
4.5g/1½ tsp	Red Chilli Powder
3g/1 tsp	*Haldee*/Turmeric Powder
3g/1 tsp	*Amchoor*/Mango Powder
	Salt

The Smoking

2	*Chhotti Elaichi*/Green Cardamom (split open)
4.5g/1 tsp	*Desi Ghee*/Clarified Butter

PREPARATION

THE CAULIFLOWER: Blanch florets in salted boiling water, drain and refresh in iced water.

THE SMOKING: Put a few small pieces of 'live' charcoal in a small *katori*/metal bowl and place the *katori*/metal bowl in a large *handi*/pan. Spread the boiled yam cubes around the *katori*/metal bowl, place cardamom on the charcoal, pour on the *ghee* and, as the smoke billows, cover with a lid and reserve for 15 minutes.

COOKING

Heat *ghee* in a *kadhai*/wok, add cumin, stir over medium heat until it begins to pop, add onions, garlic and ginger, and sauté until translucent and glossy. Then add cauliflower and smoked yam, *bhunno*/stir-fry for a minute, add *kachri*, coriander, red chilli, turmeric, *amchoor* and salt, and *bhunno*/stir-fry, adding 30ml/2 Tbs of water at regular intervals for approx 5-6 minutes. Remove and adjust the seasoning.

Bharri Harri Mirch ka Khaata

Serves: 4

Preparation Time
45 minutes

Cooking Time
20 minutes

INGREDIENTS

The *Khaata*
500g/2 cups	Yoghurt (1-day old)
30g/1 oz	*Besan*/Gramflour
225g/¾ tsp	Red Chilli Powder
1.5g/½ tsp	*Haldee*/Turmeric Powder
	Salt
50g/¼ cup	*Desi Ghee*/Clarified Butter
1g/¼ tsp	*Methidaana*/Fenugreek Seeds
2g/1 tsp	*Jeera*/Cumin Seeds
2g/½ tsp	*Rai*/Black Mustard Seeds
	A generous pinch of *Heeng*/Asafoetida

The Chilli Stuffing
12	Green Chillies
100g/3 oz	Potatoes (boil, peel & mash)
2.5g/¼" piece	Ginger (finely chop)
1.5g/½ tsp	Black Pepper (freshly roasted & coarsely ground)
1.5g/½ tsp	*Amchoor*/Mango Powder (large & plump; slit & seed)
	Salt
3.25g/1 Tbs	*Taaza Dhania*/Coriander (finely chop)

The Batter
100g/3 oz	*Besan*/Gramflour
	A pinch of Soda Bi-carb
	Salt
1.25g/½ tsp	*Ajwain*
	Cooking Oil to deep fry chillies

PREPARATION

THE KHAATA: Whisk yoghurt in a bowl, add *besan*, red chillies, turmeric and salt, and whisk to mix well. Then add 1.2 litres/5 cups of water and whisk again. (To get a *Kadhi* of better consistency, forget about yoghurt. Instead, use 1.7 litres/7 cups of *chaas*/butter milk.)

THE CHILLI FILLING: Mix all the ingredients and divide into 12 equal portions.

THE STUFFING: Pack a portion of the filling in each green chilli.

THE BATTER: Mix all the ingredients, add water (approx 45ml/3 Tbs) and mix well.

THE FRYING: Heat oil in a *kadhai*/wok, dip the stuffed chillies in the batter and deep-fry over medium heat until golden. Remove to absorbent paper to drain the excess fat.

COOKING

Heat *ghee* in a *handi*/pan, add fenugreek, cumin and mustard seeds, and stir over medium heat until they begin to pop. Add yoghurt (or buttermilk) mixture and bring to a boil, stirring continuously. Reduce to low heat, cover and simmer, stirring occasionally, until of thin sauce consistency. Then add the fried chillies, bring to a boil, reduce to low heat and simmer for 2 minutes. Remove and adjust the seasoning.

Paneer ke Sooley

Serves: 4
Preparation Time
1 hour
Cooking Time
up to 5-6 minutes

INGREDIENTS

24 piccata	Paneer (3" x 2" x ¼" cubes)

The Batter

10g/1½ Tbs	Rice Flour
6g/2 tsp	Maida/All purpose Flour
5g/2 tsp	Besan/Gramflour
60g/¼ cup	Chakka Dahi/Yoghurt Cheese/ Hung Yoghurt
20g/4 tsp	Almond Paste
15g/½ oz	Parmesan Powder (or grated)
3g/1 tsp	Red Chilli Powder
15g/5 tsp	Paneer ke Sooley Masala
	Salt
30ml/2 Tbs	Cream

The Smoking

5	Lavang/Cloves
4.5g/1 tsp	Desi Ghee/Clarified Butter

Sooley Masala

45 g	Jeera/Cumin Seeds
30g	Dhania/Coriander Seeds
8	Dry Red Chillies
4	Black Peppercorn
4	Lavang/Clove
3	Motti Elaichi/Black Cardamom
1	Jaiphal/Nutmeg
30g	Amchoor Powder
9g	Kachri Powder

Broil each whole spice separately on a *tawa*/griddle over low heat until they emit their unique aroma. Remove, cool and powder in a mixer/blender to a coarse powder. Mix *Amchoor* and *Kachri* powders and store in a plastic container.

PREPARATION

THE BATTER: Mix all the ingredients, except half the *Special Masala*, in a bowl, dip picatta in the batter and keep aside.

THE SMOKING: Put a few small pieces of 'live' charcoal in a small *katori*/metal bowl and place the *katori*/metal bowl in a large *handi*/pan. Spread the picatta around the *katori*/metal bowl, put the cloves in the *katori*/metal bowl, pour on the *ghee* and, as the smoke bellows, cover with a lid and reserve for 10 minutes.

THE SKEWERING: Carefully skewer *sooley* in convenient batches, penetrating twice, on thin skewers. Keep a tray underneath to collect drippings.

COOKING

Roast on a moderately hot charcoal grill for 5-6 minutes, basting at regular intervals.

TO SERVE

Unskewer *sooley*, arrange on platter, sprinkle reserved *Special Masala* and serve hot.

Amrud ki Subzi

Serves: 4

Preparation Time
25 minutes

Cooking Time
40 minutes

INGREDIENTS

1 kg/2¼ lb	Guavas (semi-ripe)
120/g ½ cup	Tomatoes
125g/¾ cup	Ghee
225g/1 cup	Yoghurt
5g/1¾ tsp	*Jeera*/Cumin seeds
3g/½ tsp	*Garam Masala*
A pinch	*Heeng*/Asafoetida
10g/2 tsp	Mango powder
25g/5 tsp	*Dhania*/Coriander powder
10g/2 tsp	*Saunf*/Fennel powder
3g/½ tsp	Red Chilli powder
75g/⅓ cup	Sugar
5g/1 tsp	*Haldee*/Turmeric
30ml/2 Tbs	Lemon juice
	Salt

PREPARATION

THE GUAVAS: Peel, cut into quarters deseed and halve.
THE TOMATOES: Wash and chop.
THE YOGHURT: Whisk in a bowl.

COOKING

Heat ghee in a *kadhai*, add cumin and sauté over medium heat until it begins to crackle. Add asafoetida, stir, coriander powder, red chilli, turmeric and salt. Then add the tomatoes and yoghurt, *bhunno* until the fat leaves the masala, add water (approx 250ml/1cup) and bring to a boil. Now addd guavas, bring to a boil, reduce to medium heat, cover and cook, stirring occasionally, until tender. Sprinkle garam masala, mango powder and fennel powder, stir, add sugar and cook for 5 minutes. Adjust the seasoning. Sprinkle lemon juice and stir.

TO SERVE

Remove to a dish and serve with *Poori*.

Scoop Lady Di

Serves: 4

Preparation Time
5 minutes

Cooking Time
2 hours

INGREDIENTS

3 litres/ 12½ cups	Milk
120ml/½ cup	Rose Syrup
5ml/1 tsp	Rose Water
3g/1 tsp	*Chotti Elaichi*/Green Cardamom Powder
120ml/½ cup	Cream

The Garnish

4	Spun Sugar "Birds' Nests"
4	*Chotti Elaichi*/Green Cardamom

PREPARATION
THE GREEN CARDAMOM: Peel, remove the seeds and reserve for garnish.

COOKING
Put milk in a *kadhai*/wok, bring to a boil and stir constantly for 30 minutes or until reduced to a third. Remove, cool, add rose syrup and cardamom powder, and stir until homogenous. When the *kulfi* mixture cools down to room temperature, stir-in rosewater and cream. Keep stirring until cream is fully incorporated. Now put the mixture in the gelato machine, ice-cream maker (the one that churns in the freezer of a refrigerator) or the hand-operated ice-cream bucket (apparently an electric powered version of the contraption is also available) and churn until set. You can also put the mixture in kulfi moulds and freeze them in the traditional *matka* with ice and rock salt.

TO SERVE
Arrange the "birds' nests" on each of 4 individual dessert plates, place 3 scoops of kulfi in each, sprinkle equal quantities of cardamom seeds on top and serve immediately.

The Merchant Princes' *Bhoj*

Arbi ke Kebab

Serves: 4

Preparation Time
1:30 hours

Cooking Time
5 minutes/set

INGREDIENTS

1 Kg/2¼ lb	*Arbi*/Coloccasia (2" long)
	Cooking Oil to deep-fry
25g/2 Tbs	*Desi Ghee*/Clarified Butter
3g/1½ tsp	*Jeera*/Cumin Seeds
20g/3 Tbs	Flour of Roasted *Channa*/Bengal Gram
	Salt
1.5g/½ tsp	Red Chilli Powder
5g/½" piece	Ginger (chop)
4	Green Chillies (chop)
5g/4½ tsp	*Dhania*/Coriander (chop)
2.25g/¾ tsp	Black Pepper (freshly roasted & coarsely ground)
	A tiny pinch of *Chhotti Elaichi*/Green Cardamom Powder
	A tiny pinch of *Motti Elaichi*/Black Cardamom Powder
	A tiny pinch of *Lavang*/Clove Powder
	A tiny pinch of *Daalcheeni*/Cinnamon Powder
	A tiny pinch of *Gulaab Pankhri*/Rose Petal Powder
	A tiny pinch of *Jaiphal*/Nutmeg Powder
	Arraroot/Cornflour to dust

The Bouquet Garni

8	*Lavang*/Cloves
4	*Chhotti Elaichi*/Green Cardamom
2	*Motti Elaichi*/Black Cardamom
¼	*Jaiphal*/Nutmeg

The Filling

100g/3 oz	*Khoya*
100g/3 oz	Roasted Cashewnuts (broken)
15g/½ oz	Raisins
5g/½" piece	Ginger (chop)
1.5g/½ tsp	*Dhania*/Coriander (chop)
2	Green Chillies (chop)
	A generous pinch of *Amchoor*/Mango Powder
	A pinch of *Kaala Namak*/Black Rock Salt Powder
	A pinch of *Jeera*/Cumin Powder
	A pinch of *Kasoori Methi*/Fenugreek Powder

PREPARATION

THE *ARBI*/COLOCCASIA: Wash, put in a *handi*/pan, add the bouquet garni and boil until soft but not squishy (approx 15 minutes), drain, cool, peel and keep aside. Heat oil in a *kadhai*/wok, add the boiled *arbi* and deep-fry over medium heat until lightly coloured. Remove to absorbent paper to drain excess fat. Then mash, ensuring there are no lumps. Reserve the oil.

Melt *ghee* in a *kadhai*/wok, add cumin, stir over medium heat until it begins to pop, add the mashed *arbi* and *bhunno*/stir-fry for 5-6 minutes. Then add red chilli powder and flour of roasted *channa* and *bhunno*/stir-fry until the moisture has completely evaporated and the *arbi* mixture becomes like a *khoya* ball. Remove and spread on a flat surface to cool immediately. Now add the ginger, green chillies, coriander and the powdered spices, mix well, adjust the seasoning and divide into 16 equal portions and make balls.

THE FILLING: Put *khoya* in a heavy bottom *kadhai*/wok and *bhunno* until lightly coloured. (Ensure that the *khoya* doesn't become brown or burnt.) Transfer to a bowl, add the remaining ingredients, mix well and divide into 16 equal portions.

THE STUFFING: Flatten each ball between the palms, place a portion of the filling in the middle, make balls again and flatten into ¾" thick round patties. Dust with corn flour and keep aside.

COOKING

Re-heat the reserved oil, add the patties and deep-fry over medium heat until golden and crisp. Remove to absorbent paper to drain the excess fat.

TO SERVE

Remove to a service dish, garnish with green chillies, lemon wedges and serve with coriander chutney.

Jaipuri Subz Seekh

Serves: 4
Preparation Time: 1:30 hours
Cooking Time: 3-4 minutes

INGREDIENTS

500g/1 lb 2 oz	*Arbi*/Coloccasia (2" long)
180g/6 oz	Paneer (grate)
120g/¼ lb	Khoya (grate)
5g/2 Tbs	*Taaza Pudhina*/Mint (chop)
10g/1" piece	Ginger (finely chop)
6	Green Chillies (seed & finely chop)
3g/1 tsp	*Anaardana*/Pomegranate Seed Powder
	A generous pinch of *Kasoori Methi*/Dried Fenugreek Leaf Powder
	Salt

The *Bouquet Garni* for Colocassia

8	*Lavang*/Cloves
4	*Chhotti Elaichi*/Green Cardamom
2	*Motti Elaichi*/Black Cardamom
¼	*Jaiphal*/Nutmeg

The *Subz Seekh* Masala

15g/5 tsp	Amchoor
3g/1 tsp	Black Pepper (freshly roasted & coarsely ground)
3g/1 tsp	*Jeera*/Cumin Powder
1.5g/½ tsp	*Chhotti Elaichi*/Green Cardamom Powder
1.5g/½ tsp	*Javitri*/Mace Powder
1.5g/½ tsp	*Kaala Namak*/Black Rock Salt Powder

PREPARATION

THE *ARBI*/COLOCCASIA: Wash, put in a *handi*/pan, add the *bouquet garni* and boil until soft but not squishy (approx 15 minutes), drain, cool, peel and mash, ensuring there is no lumps. Discard the *bouquet garni*.

THE *SEEKH* MIXTURE: Put all the ingredients in a bowl, add the masala, mix well, mash, divide into 12 equal portions and make balls.

THE SKEWERING: Using a moist hand, spread the balls by pressing each along the length of the skewers, two inches apart and making each *kebab* 4 inches long.

COOKING

Roast in a moderately hot tandoor for 3-4 minutes or until golden. On a charcoal grill for about the same time.

TO SERVE

Unskewer, arrange on a platter, sprinkle a generous pinch or two the *Subz Seekh Masala* and serve hot with mint chutney or fresh mango chutney or *saunth*.

Aloo ki Tehree

Serves: 4

Preparation Time
1 hour

Cooking Time
45 minutes

INGREDIENTS

The Potatoes

6	Potatoes (medium)
1.5g/½ tsp	*Haldee*/Turmeric Powder
1.5g/½ tsp	Yellow Chilli Powder
	Salt
	Cooking Oil to deep-fry

The Rice

300g/1½ cups	*Basmati* Rice
15ml/1 Tbs	Lemon Juice
7.5g/¾" piece	Ginger
2	Green Chillies
3g/1 tsp	*Haldee*/Turmeric Powder
1.5g/½ tsp	*Chhotti Elaichi*/Green Cardamom Powder
24	Black Peppercorns
2 drops	*Kewra*

The Bouquet Garni

5g/2 tsp	*Saunf*/Fennel Seeds
5	*Chhotti Elaichi*/Green Cardamom
4	*Motti Elaichi*/Black Cardamom
4	*Lavang*/Cloves
2	*Tej Patta*/Bay Leaf
2 sticks	*Daalcheeni*/Cinnamon (1")

The *Jhol*/Liquor

120ml/½ cup	Vegetable Stock
60ml/2 oz	Yoghurt
40g/3 Tbs	*Desi Ghee*/Clarified Butter
2g/1 tsp	*Jeera*/Cumin Seeds
2.25g/¾ tsp	Yellow Chilli Powder
15ml/1 Tbs	Lemon Juice
	Salt

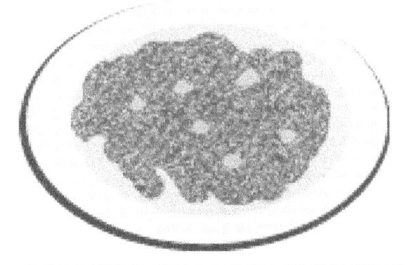

PREPARATION

THE POTATOES: Peel potatoes, wash, quarter and pat dry. Boil enough water in *handi*/pan, add turmeric, yellow chillies and salt, stir, add potatoes and boil until half cooked, drain and pat dry.

Heat oil in a *kadhai*/wok, add the potatoes and deep-fry until light golden. Remove to absorbent paper to drain excess fat.

THE RICE: Pick rice, wash in running water, drain and soak for 45 minutes. Drain at the time of cooking. Scrape, wash and cut ginger into juliennes. Wash green chillies, slit, seed, cut into strips and discard the stems.

THE BOUQUET GARNI: Put ingredients in mortar and pound with pestle to break spices, fold in piece of muslin and secure with enough string for it to hang over rim of *handi*/pan.

THE *JHOL*/LIQUOR: Whisk yoghurt in a bowl. Heat *ghee* in a large *handi*/pan, add cumin seeds, stir until they begin to crackle, add stock, bring to boil over medium heat, reduce to very low heat, add yoghurt and the remaining ingredients, stir, simmer for 5 minutes, remove and keep aside.

COOKING

To cook the rice, boil 1.5litres/6¼ cups litres of water in *handi*/pan, add *bouquet garni* and salt, stir, add rice, bring to boil, reduce to medium heat, add lemon juice and continue to boil, stirring occasionally, until nine-tenths cooked. Drain, discard *bouquet garni* and keep aside.

ASSEMBLING

Put half the *jhol*/liquor in *handi*/pan, spread a third of boiled rice and arrange half the fried potatoes evenly on top. Spread another third of rice and arrange remaining fried potatoes evenly on top. Spread remaining rice, pour on remaining *jhol*/liquor, cover with lid, seal with *atta* (whole wheat) dough and cook over low heat for 25-30 minutes. Remove.

TO SERVE

Break seal and serve from *handi*/pan itself with *Raita*.

Baingan Bemisaal

Serves: 4
Preparation Time: 1:15 hours
Cooking Time: 30 minutes

INGREDIENTS

4		Baingan/Aubergines (large; round)
		Cooking Oil to grease roasting tray
		Cooking Oil to deep-fry

The Filling

500g/1lb 2 oz	Kid Mince
50g/¼ cup	Unsalted Butter
15ml/1 Tbs	Cooking Oil
90g/3 oz	Onions
25g/4 tsp	Garlic Paste (strain)
15g/2½ tsp	Ginger Paste (strain)
8g/1 Tbs	Fresh Fennel
240ml/1 cup	Clear Kid/Lamb Stock
150g/5 oz	Fresh Tomato Purée
1g/2 tsp	Van Ajwain/Thyme (dried)
1.5g/½ tsp	Red Chilli Powder
	Salt
24	Green Peppercorns (fresh if you can obtain them)
16	Roasted Pistachios
75g/2½ oz	Paneer
45g/1½ oz	Cheddar Cheese
15g/½ oz	Khoya
2.25g/¾ tsp	Chhotti Elaichi/Green Cardamom Powder
1.5g/½ tsp	Javitri/Mace Powder

PREPARATION

THE AUBERGINES: Wash and halve. Heat oil in a *kadhai*/deep-frying pan, add aubergines and deep-fry for 2 minutes. Remove, cool, carefully scoop out the pulp, leaving half an inch, to make "moulds" and keep aside. (Use the pulp to make *Bhartha* as an accompanying dish.)

THE FILLING: Peel, wash and finely chop onions. Remove the whiskers and the outer layer, wash and finely chop leeks and fennel. Wash and pat dry green peppercorns. (If using canned peppercorns, drain and pat dry.)

Grate *paneer*, cheddar and *khoya* in a bowl, and mix well.

Heat butter and oil in a frying pan, add onions and leeks, sauté over medium heat until onions are light golden, add garlic and ginger pastes, sauté until onions are golden, add fennel and stir. Then add mince, *bhunno*/stir-fry for 2-3 minutes, add 240ml/1 cup of stock, bring to a boil, reduce to low heat and simmer, stirring occasionally, until the liquid has evaporated. Increase to medium heat and *bhunno*/stir-fry until the fat leaves the sides. Now add tomato purée, thyme, red chillies and salt, *bhunno*/stir-fry until the fat leaves the sides again. Sprinkle green cardamom and mace, stir, remove, adjust the seasoning (keeping in mind that you will be adding cheese later) and divide into 8 equal portions.

THE STUFFING: Put a portion of the filling in the aubergine "moulds", cover with equal quantities of the *paneer*, cheddar and khoya mixture, arrange in a greased roasting tray and keep aside.

THE GRAVY: Clean curry leaves, wash and pat dry. Remove eyes, wash and roughly chop tomatoes. Peel, wash and roughly chop onions. Remove the whiskers and the outer layer, wash and roughly chop leeks. Peel and roughly chop garlic. Wash red chillies, slit, seed, roughly chop and discard the stems.

Put the flour of roasted gram in a bowl, add the butter, mix until homogenous and refrigerate.

THE OVEN: Pre-heat to 275°F.

The Gravy

750g/1lb/11 oz	Tomatoes
60ml/¼ cup	Cooking Oil (preferably olive oil)
16	Curry Leaves
65g/½ cup	Onions
65g/½ cup	Leeks
8 flakes	Garlic
2	Bay Leaves
8	Black Peppercorns
4.5g/3 Tbs	*Van Ajwain*/Thyme (dried)
2	Fresh Red Chillies
1 litre/4¼ cups	Clear Kid/Lamb Stock
	Salt
5.25g/2 tsp	Flour of Roasted Gram
5.25g/1¼ tsp	Unsalted Butter

COOKING

Put the roasting tray in the pre-heated oven and bake for 7-8 minutes, then turn on the top heat and bake for 2 minutes or until the cheese is lightly coloured.

To prepare the gravy, heat oil in a pot, add curry leaves, stir over medium heat for a few seconds, add onions and leeks, sauté until onions are translucent, add garlic and sauté until onions are light golden, add bay leaves and peppercorns, sauté until onions are golden. Then add tomatoes, cover and cook, stirring occasionally, until mashed, add stock, bring to a boil, reduce to low heat and simmer, stirring occasionally, until reduced by half. Remove and pass through a fine mesh soup strainer into a *handi*/pan. Return gravy to heat, add thyme, red chillies and salt, stir and simmer, stirring occasionally until of ketchup consistency. Spinkle cardamom and mace, stir, remove and adjust the seasoning.

TO SERVE

Make a bed of sauce on a third each of four plates, arrange two stuffed aubergines on the sauce and serve with sautéed potatoes, carrots and beans.

Baingan ki Launj

Serves: 4
Preparation Time 1 hour
Cooking Time 20 minutes

INGREDIENTS

24	*Baingan*/Eggplant/Brinjals (small; oblong)
	Salt
75g/6 Tbs	*Desi Ghee*/Clarified Butter
2	*Lavang*/Cloves
120g/4 oz	*Gurh*/Jaggery (grate)
60ml/¼ cup	Lemon Juice
	A pinch of Black Pepper (freshly roasted & coarsely ground)
	A pinch of *Lavang*/Clove Powder
	A pinch of *Daalcheeni*/Cinnamon Powder
	A pinch of *Motti Elaichi*/Black Cardamom Powder

The Filling

150g/5 oz	Onions (slice)
	Desi Ghee/Clarified Butter to deep fry onions
25g/2½" piece	Ginger (finely chop)
9g/1 Tbs	Red Chilli Powder
6g/2 tsp	Black Pepper (freshly roasted & coarsely ground)
	A pinch of *Lavang*/Clove Powder
	A pinch of *Daalcheeni*/Cinnamon Powder
	A pinch of *Motti Elaichi*/Black Cardamom Powder

PREPARATION

THE EGGPLANT: Make a slit on one side to create pockets, rub in salt and reserve for 30 minutes.

THE FILLING: Heat *ghee* in a *kadhai*/wok, add onions and deep-fry over medium heat until golden and crisp. Remove to absorbent paper to drain excess fat. When cool, crush to make a coarse powder, add the remaining ingredients, mix well, and divide into 24 equal portions. Reserve the *ghee*.

THE STUFFING: Pack a portion of the filling in each eggplant and secure with string (to prevent the filling from spilling out).

THE JAGGERY: Reserve in lemon juice.

COOKING

Melt 75g/6 Tbs of the reserved *ghee* in a *kadhai*/wok, add cloves and stir over medium heat for 30 seconds. Then add stuffed eggplant, reduce to low heat, cover and cook, turning over at regular intervals, until cooked (approx 10 minutes). Uncover, add jaggery, along with lemon juice, cover and cook on *dum*, turning occasionally, until the masala nappes the eggplant. Now sprinkle pepper, clove, cinnamon and black cardamom powders, stir, remove and adjust the seasoning.

TO SERVE

Remove string, arrange on a platter and serve as an accompaniment.

Bharwaan Parwal

Serves: 4
Preparation Time 1 hour
Cooking Time 20 minutes

INGREDIENTS

16	*Parwal*/Wax Gourd (medium)
	Cooking oil to deep-fry

The Marination

30ml/2 Tbs	Lemon Juice
4.5g/1½ tsp	Red Chilli Powder
3g/1 tsp	*Haldee*/Turmeric Powder
	Salt

The Filling

150g/5 oz	*Paneer*
75g/1½ oz	Potatoes
10g/1" piece	Ginger
3.25g/1 Tbs	*Taaza Dhania*/Coriander
2	Green Chillies
6g/2 tsp	*Amchoor*/Mango Powder
3g/1 tsp	Black Pepper Powder (freshly broiled & coarsely ground)
32	Cashew Nut Halves
	Salt

The Gravy

25g/2 Tbs	*Desi Ghee*/Clarified Butter
3g/1½ tsp	*Jeera*/Cumin Seeds
	A generous pinch *Heeng*/Asafoetida
250g/7 oz	Yoghurt
15g/5 tsp	*Dhania*/Coriander Powder
3g/1 tsp	Red Chilli Powder
3g/1 tsp	*Haldee*/Turmeric Powder
150g/5 oz	Tomatoes
30g/2 Tbs	Roasted Cashew Nut Paste
720ml/3 cups	Vegetable Stock (or water)
	Salt
1.5g/½ tsp	*Chhotti Elaichi*/Green Cardamom Powder
0.75g/¼ tsp	*Lavang*/Clove Powder
0.75g/¼ tsp	*Daalcheeni*/Cinnamon Powder
0.75g/¼ tsp	*Javitri*/Mace Powder

The Garnish

15g/½ oz	*Paneer*
15g/½ oz	Flakes of Toasted Almonds
1	Tomato (large)

PREPARATION

THE *PARWAL*: Wash, peel, cut from one end, core the length of each *parwal*, leaving ¼" walls to form "tubes".

THE MARINATION: Mix all the ingredients and rub the *parwal*—inside and out—with this marinade. Keep aside for 15 minutes.

THE FRYING: Heat oil in a *kadhai*/wok and deep-fry the marinated *parwal* over medium heat until cooked (approx 5-7 minutes). The *parwal* will become limp but that is no cause for worry! Remove to absorbent paper to drain the excess fat.

THE FILLING: Grate *paneer* and cheese in a bowl. Boil, cool, peel and dice potatoes (ensure that the potatoes are not over-cooked). Scrape, wash and finely chop ginger. Clean, wash and finely chop coriander. Wash green chillies, slit, seed, finely chop and discard the stems. Mix these and the remaining ingredients with the *paneer*, divide into 16 equal portions.

THE STUFFING: Stuff a portion of the filling in each *parwal*, compressing to ensure it is firmly packed.

THE GRAVY: Reserve asafoetida in 15ml/1 Tbs of water. Whisk yoghurt in a bowl, add coriander, red chilli and turmeric powders, whisk again to mix well. Remove eyes, wash and roughly chop tomatoes.

THE GARNISH: Grate *paneer* in a bowl. Remove eyes, wash, quarter, remove the pulp and the seeds, and dice.

COOKING

Heat *ghee* in a *handi*/pan, add cumin seeds, stir over medium heat until they begin to pop, add asafoetida, stir until it puffs up, remove *handi*/pan from heat, stir in the yoghurt mixture, return *handi*/pan to heat and *bhunno*/stir-fry until the fat leaves the sides. Then add the tomatoes, *bhunno*/stir-fry until the fat leaves the sides, add cashew nut paste and *bhunno*/stir-fry until the fat leaves the sides. Now add the stock, bring to a boil, reduce to low heat, simmer, stirring occasionally, until the stock is reduced by a third, add the stuffed *parwal* and simmer, stirring occasionally—and carefully, for 5-6 minutes or until the gravy is of medium thick consistency. Sprinkle green cardamom, clove, cinnamon and mace powders, stir, remove and adjust the seasoning.

TO SERVE

Remove the *parwal* to a serving dish, pour on the gravy, garnish with grated *paneer*, toasted almonds and tomato dices. Serve with *Poori* or *Phulka*.

Bhunney Bharree Badhi Mirch

Serves: 4
Preparation Time 1:30 hours
Cooking Time 5-6 minutes

INGREDIENTS

12	*Harri Shimla Mirch*/Green Bell Peppers

The Filling
200g/7 oz	Potatoes
200g/7 oz	Button Mushrooms
60g/2 oz	Carrots
30ml/2 Tbs	Cooking Oil
60g/½ cup	Onions
10g/1½ Tbs	*Besan*/Gramflour
10g/1" piece	Ginger
5g/4½ tsp	*Taaza Dhania*/Coriander
2	Green Chillies
	A pinch of *Motti Elaichi*/Black Cardamom
	A pinch of *Dhania*/Coriander Powder
	A pinch of *Saunf*/Fennel Powder
36	Cashewnuts (golden fried)
36	Raisins
	Salt
30ml/2 Tbs	Lemon Juice
60g/2 oz	Paneer

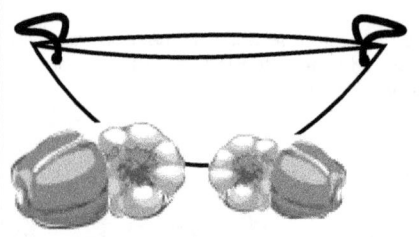

PREPARATION

THE CAPSICUM: Remove the caps, carefully seed, wash and wipe dry.

THE FILLING: Boil potatoes, cool, peel and cut into 3" cubes. Remove the earthy base of the stalks, wash in running water, blanch in salted boiling water for 2 minutes, drain, cool immediately, quarter and pat dry. Peel carrots, wash, dice, blanch in salted boiling water for 2 minutes, drain, cool immediately and pat dry. Peel, wash and finely chop onions. Scrape, wash and finely chop ginger. Clean, wash and finely chop coriander. Remove stems, wash, slit, seed and finely chop green chillies. Clean raisins, remove stems, soak in water, drain and pat dry. Grate *paneer*.

Heat oil in a *kadhai*/wok, add onions, sauté over medium heat until light brown, add *besan*/gramflour, and *bhunno*/stir-fry until it emits its unique aroma (approx 12-2 minutes). Add potatoes, *bhunno*/stir-fry for two minutes, add the remaining ingredients, except lemon juice, cashewnuts, a quarter of the raisins and *paneer*, *bhunno*/stir-fry for a minute. Remove, cool, add lemon juice, mix well, adjust the seasoning and divide into 12 equal portions.

THE STUFFING: Stuff a portion of the filling in each capsicum, compressing to ensure it is firmly packed.

THE OVEN: Pre-heat to 275°F.

COOKING

The *kebab* can be cooked in 2 ways:
1. Pierce 3 capsicum sideways on each of 4 individual skewers and grill over medium heat for 5-6 minutes, brushing with butter a couple of times.
2. Grease a roasting tray with oil, arrange the stuffed capsicum in it and roast in the pre-heated oven for 7-8 minutes.

To Serve

Serve with a garnish of equal quantities of cashewnuts, the remaining raisins and the grated *paneer*.

Dhania Khumb Mongodi

Serves: 4

Preparation Time
45 minutes

Cooking Time
15 minutes

INGREDIENTS

250g/9 oz	*Taaza Dhania*/Coriander (coarsely chop)
16	Button Mushrooms (quarter)
150g/5 oz	*Mongodi* (*Urad Daal*)
	Cooking Oil to deep-fry *Mongodi*
65g/5 Tbs	*Desi Ghee*/Clarified Butter
4g/2 tsp	*Jeera*/Cumin Seeds
20g/3½ tsp	Ginger Paste (strain)
10g/1¾ tsp	Garlic Paste (strain)
15g/5 tsp	*Dhania*/Coriander Powder
3g/1 tsp	Red Chilli Powder
15g/5 tsp	*Haldee*/Turmeric Powder
240g/1 cup	Fresh Tomato Purée
2.25g/¾ tsp	Black Pepper Powder (freshly & coarsely ground)
1.5g/½ tsp	*Chhotti Elaichi*/Green Cardamom Powder
0.75g/¼ tsp	*Daalcheeni*/Cinnamon Powder
0.75g/¼ tsp	*Jaiphal*/Nutmeg Powder
	A generous pinch of *Kasoori Methi*/Fenugreek Powder

PREPARATION

THE *MONGODI*: Heat oil in a *kadhai*/wok, add the *mongodi* and deep-fry until golden. Remove to absorbent paper to drain excess fat and then reserve in a panful of water until ready to cook.

COOKING

Heat *ghee* in a *kadhai*/wok, add cumin seeds, stir over medium heat until they begin to pop, add garlic and ginger pastes, *bhunno*/stir-fry until the moisture evaporates, add the fresh, chopped coriander, *bhunno*/stir-fry until the moisture evaporates add coriander, red chilli and turmeric powders (dissolved in 60ml/3 cup of water) and *bhunno*/stir-fry until the moisture evaporates. Then add tomato purée, *bhunno*/stir-fry until the fat leaves the sides, add mushrooms, *mongodi* and salt, *bhunno*/stir-fry for 5-7 minutes or until the coriander nappes mushrooms and *mongodi*. Sprinkle pepper, green cardamom, cinnamon, nutmeg and *kasoori methi* powders, stir, remove and adjust the seasoning.

Maaweywale Aloo

Serves: 4
Preparation Time 1:15 hours
Cooking Time 25 minutes

INGREDIENTS

12	Potatoes (medium)
	Cooking Oil to deep-fry potatoes

The Filling

100g/3 oz	*Khoya* (grate)
100g/3 oz	*Paneer* (grate)
10g/1" piece	Ginger (finely chop)
3	Green Chillies (seed & finely chop)
3.25g/1 Tbs	*Taaza Dhania*/Coriander (chop)
30g/1 oz	*Anaar*/Pomegranate
	Salt

The Gravy

100g/3 oz	*Desi Ghee*/Clarified Butter
5	*Chhotti Elaichi*/Green Cardamom
3	*Motti Elaichi*/Black Cardamom
3	*Lavang*/Cloves
2g/1 tsp	*Jeera*/Cumin Seeds
	A generous pinch of *Heeng*/Asafoetida
30g/5 tsp	Ginger Paste (strain)
20g/7 tsp	*Dhania*/Coriander Powder
4.5g/1½ tsp	*Laal Mirch*/Red Chilli Powder
4.5g/1½ tsp	*Haldee*/Turmeric Powder
500ml/2 cups	Fresh Tomato Purée
	Salt
4.5g/1½ tsp	Black Pepper (freshly roasted & coarsely ground)
30g/2 Tbs	Cashewnut Paste

PREPARATION

THE POTATOES: Peel, wash, make barrel shapes and scoop out the centre leaving ¼" walls on the sides and the base intact. Heat oil in a *kadhai*/wok and deep-fry over medium heat until cooked and light brown in colour. Remove to absorbent paper to drain excess fat and cool.

THE FILLING: Mix all the ingredients and divide into 12 equal portions.

THE STUFFING: Pack a portion of the filling in each potato 'barrel'.

COOKING

Heat *ghee* in a *handi*/pan, add green cardamom, black cardamom and cloves, stir over medium heat until the green cardamom changes colour, add cumin, stir until it begins to pop, add asafoetida and stir until it puffs up. Then add ginger paste (alongwith 120ml/2 cups of water), stir over medium heat until the moisture evaporates, add coriander, red chilli and turmeric powders (dissolved in 60ml/3 cups of water) and stir until the moisture evaporates. Now tomato purée and *bhunno*/stir-fry until the fat leaves the sides, add the cashew paste, *bhunno*/stir-fry until the fat leaves the sides, add water (approx 720ml/3 cups), bring to a boil, reduce to low heat and simmer, stirring occasionally, for 2-3 minutes. Remove and pass the gravy through a fine mesh sieve into a separate *handi*/pan, return to heat, add the stuffed potatoes and simmer, stirring occasionally, until of thin sauce consistency.

Malaai Kofta

Serves: 4

Preparation Time
1:45 hours

Cooking Time
25 minutes

INGREDIENTS

The *Kofta*
600g/1 lb 5 oz	*Paneer*/Cottage Cheese
50g /⅓ cup	Flour
	Cooking Oil to deep-fry *kofta*

The Filling
150g /5 oz	*Malaai*/Clotted Cream
150g/ 5 oz	*Paneer*/Cottage Cheese
30g/1 oz	Khoya
3.25g/ 1 Tbs	*Taaza Dhania*/Coriander
5g/½" piece	Ginger
2.5g/1 tsp	*Shahi Jeera*/Black or Royal Cumin Seeds
16	Cashew Nut Halves
16	Raisins
0.5g/1 tsp	Saffron
15ml/1 Tbs	Milk
	Salt

The Gravy
45g/3½ Tbs	*Desi Ghee* (Clarified Butter)
3	*Chhotti Elaichi*/Green Cardamom
2	*Lavang*/Cloves
1	*Motti Elaichi*/Black Cardamom
2	*Tej Patta*/Bay Leaf
1 stick	*Daalcheeni*/Cinnamon (1")
20g/3½ tsp	Ginger Paste (strain)
3g/1 Tbs	*Dhania*/Coriander Powder
3g/1 tsp	*Kashmiri Deghi Mirch* Powder
20g/1½ Tbs	Cashew Nut Paste
750g/1 lb 11 oz	Tomatoes
1 litre/4½ cups	Vegetable Stock
	Salt
1.5g/½ tsp	*Chhotti Elaichi*/Green Cardamom Powder
0.75g/¼ tsp	*Javitri*/Mace Powder
0.375g/⅛ tsp	*Lavang*/Clove Powder
0.375g/⅛ tsp	*Daalcheeni*/Cinnamon Powder

PREPARATION

THE KOFTA MIXTURE: Mash *paneer* (cottage cheese) in a bowl, add flour and mix. Divide into 8 equal portions and make balls.

THE FILLING: Grate *paneer*, and khoya and then mash with the base of your palm. Clean, wash and finely chop coriander. Scrape, wash and finely chop ginger. Crush saffron threads with a pestle or the back of spoon, reserve in lukewarm milk for 15 minutes and then make a paste. Put these and the remaining ingredients in a bowl, mix well and divide into 8 equal portions, ensuring each portion has an equal number of cashew nut halves and raisins.

THE STUFFING: Flatten the *paneer* balls between the palms, place a portion of the filling in the middle and make oval shaped *kofta*.

THE KOFTA: Heat oil in a *kadhai*/wok, add the stuffed *kofta* and deep-fry over medium heat until golden. Remove to absorbent paper to drain excess fat.

THE GRAVY: Remove eyes, wash and finely chop tomatoes. Clean, wash and chop basil.

COOKING

Heat ghee in a *handi*/pan, add green cardamom, cloves, black cardamom, bay leaves and cinnamon, stir over medium heat until the green cardamom begins to change colour. Add the ginger paste, *bhunno*/stir-fry for a minute, add coriander powder and *Kashmiri deghi mirch* (both dissolved in 45ml/3 Tbs of water), stir until the liquid evaporates. Then add cashew nut paste, stir until the fat leaves the sides, add tomatoes and bring to a boil, reduce to low heat and simmer until tomatoes are cooked and mashed. Now add stock, bring to a boil, reduce to low heat and simmer until of thin sauce consistency. Remove and pass the gravy through fine mesh soup strainer into a separate *handi*/pan. Return the gravy to heat, gently add the fried *kofta* and simmer until the gravy is of sauce consistency (approx. 5 minutes). Sprinkle cardamom, mace, clove and cinnamon powders and stir carefully. Remove and adjust the seasoning.

TO SERVE

Place 2 *kofta* in the middle of each of 4 individual plates, pour on equal quantities of the gravy and serve with *Chappati* or *Phulka*.

Rasgulley ki Subzi

Serves: 4
Preparation Time 15 minutes
Cooking Time 8-10 minutes

INGREDIENTS

12	Rasgulley (squeeze out the syrup and reserve in water)
100g/ 3 oz	*Desi Ghee*/Clarified Butter
30g/ 5 tsp	Ginger Paste (strain)
3g/1 tsp	*Jeera*/Cumin Powder
120ml/½ cups	Yoghurt
20g/7 tsp	*Dhania*/Coriander Powder
6g/2 tsp	Tonk *Laal Mirch*/Red Chilli Powder
4.5g/1½ tsp	*Haldee*/Turmeric Powder
	Salt
30g/2 Tbs	*Chaar Magaz* Paste
420ml/1¾ cups	Fresh Tomato Purée
1.5g/½ tsp	*Motti Elaichi*/Black Cardamom Powder
0.75g/¼ tsp	*Javitri*/Mace Powder
0.75g/¼ tsp	*Gulaab Pankhrhi*/Rose Petal Powder

The Tempering
12.5g/1 Tbs	*Desi Ghee*/Clarified Butter

PREPARATION

THE YOGHURT MIXTURE: Put yoghurt in a bowl, add coriander powder, red chillies, turmeric and salt, and whisk to obtain a homogenous mixture.

COOKING

Heat *ghee* in a *handi*/pan, add ginger paste (along with 120ml/½ cup of water), stir over medium heat until the moisture evaporates. Remove *handi*/pan from heat, add the yoghurt mixture, return *handi*/pan to heat and *bhunno*/stir-fry until the fat leaves the sides. Add *chaar magaz* paste, *bhunno*/stir-fry until the fat leaves the sides, add tomato purée and *bhunno*/stir-fry until the fat leaves the sides. Then add water (approx 360ml/1½ cups), bring to a boil, reduce to low heat, drain and add *Rasgulley*, bring to a boil, reduce to low heat and simmer, stirring occasionally, for 2 minutes. Sprinkle cumin, cardamom, mace and rose petal powders, stir, remove and adjust the seasoning.

Khad Murg

Bati

Mongodi ki Subzi

Lal Maas

Khad

Murg ke Sooley

Khadhe Masaley ka Murg

Maalgoba

Safaed Maas

Gol Maas Kaacher

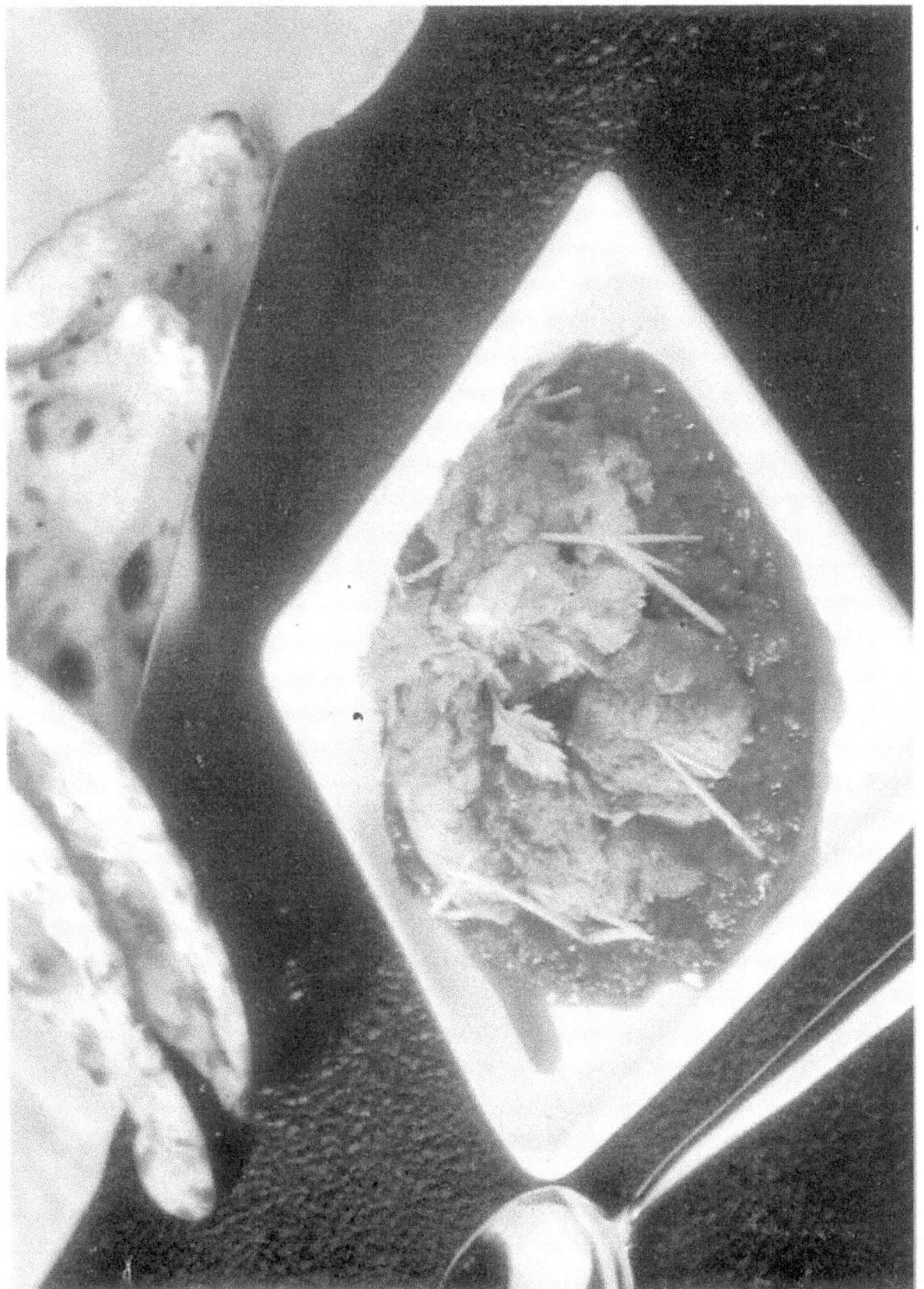

Adlah

Gobhi Rajwadi

Amrud ki Subzi

Malaai Kofta

Kandhey ki Subzi

Methi Kishmish

Heeng Jeerey ke Aloo

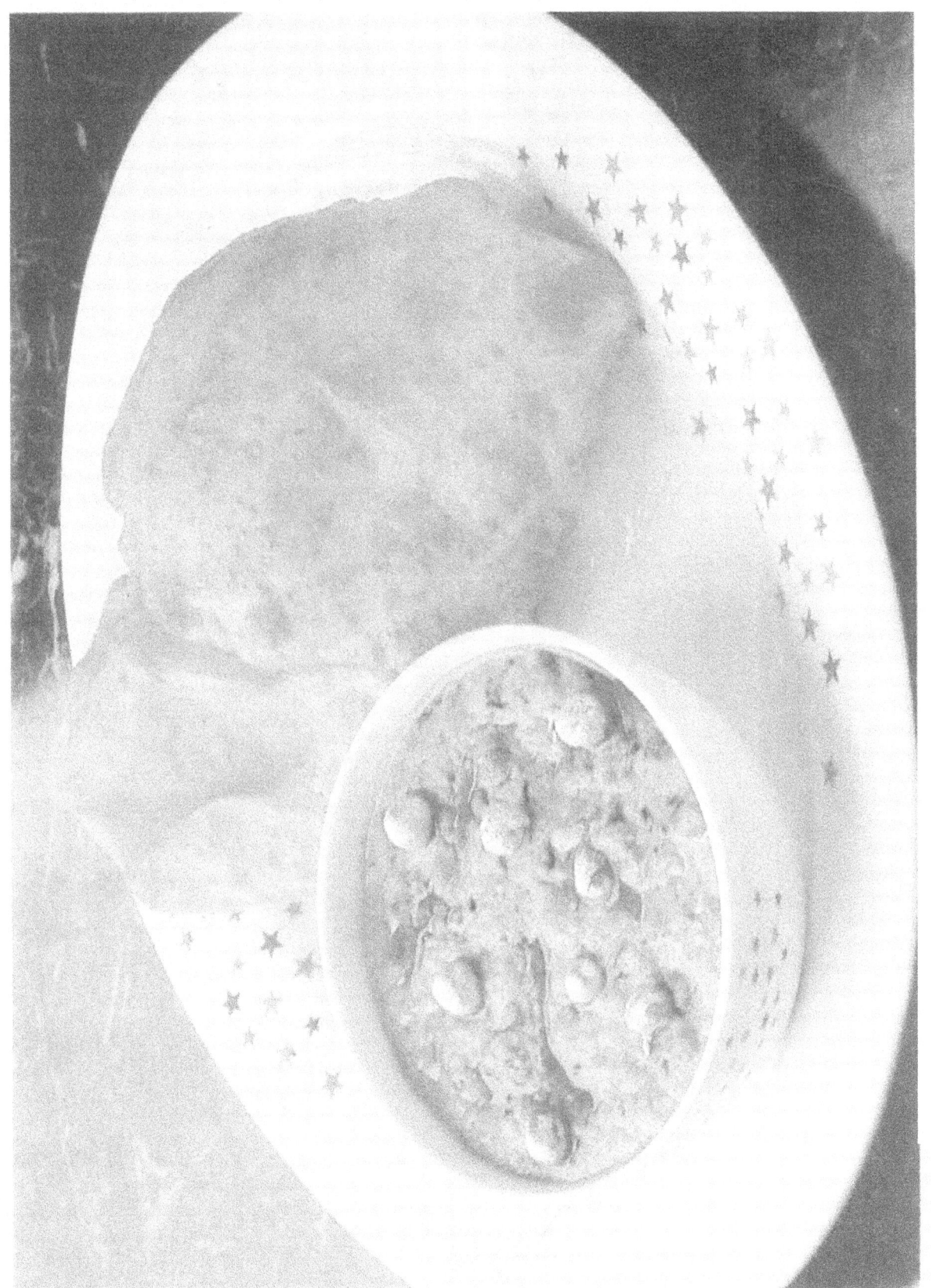

Mawa Muttar

Moong Dal Khilma

Chandrakaar Paneer

Serves: 4
Preparation Time 1:30 hours
Cooking Time 45 minutes

INGREDIENTS

16 roundels	*Paneer* (2" diameter; ¼" thick)
	Cooking oil to deep-fry

The Filling

60g/2 oz	Button Mushrooms
110g/¼ lb	Broccoli
45g/1½ oz	Carrots
1	*Laal Shimla Mirch*/Red Bell Pepper
60g/2 oz	Cheese (Parmesan/Cheddar)
30g/1 oz	Butter
3g/1½ tsp	Caraway or *Ajwain* Seeds
3g/1 tsp	Black Pepper (freshly roasted & coarsely ground)
	Salt

The Batter

75g/2½ oz	Flour
30g/1 oz	*Sooji*/Semolina
	Salt

The Gravy

500g/3 cups	Tomatoes
60ml/¼ cup	Cooking Oil
5g/½" piece	Ginger Powder or Paprika
4 flakes	Garlic
8	Black Peppercorns
2	*Tej Patta*/Bay Leaf
	A few sprigs *Soya/Sua*/Dill
1.5g/½ tsp	Kashmiri *Deghi Mirch*
0.75g/¼ tsp	*Lavang*/Clove Powder
0.75g/¼ tsp	*Jaiphal*/Nutmeg Powder
	Salt

PREPARATION

THE *PANEER*: Halve the roundels and trim.

THE FILLING: Slice the earthy lower bit of the stalks of mushrooms, wash in running water to remove grit, drain, reserve in water and finely chop at the time of cooking. Remove stems, wash and cut broccoli into tiny florets. Peel, wash and cut carrots into the smallest possible dices. Remove stem, wash, quarter, seed and cut red pepper/capsicum into the brunnoise (smallest possible dices).

Melt butter in a frying pan, add mushrooms and carrots, stir over medium heat for 2-3 minutes, add broccoli and cook until devoid of moisture, add red pepper, stir for a few seconds, remove and cool. Put all the ingredients in a bowl, mix well and divide into 16 equal portions.

THE STUFFING: Place half the paneer halves on a work surface, spread a portion of the filling evenly on top, cover with the remaining halves to make "sandwiches" and keep aside.

THE BATTER: Pick, wash and soak semolina. Sift flour and salt, add semolina and 45ml/3 Tbs of water and make a smooth batter.

THE GRAVY: Remove eyes, wash and roughly chop tomatoes. Scrape, wash and chop ginger. Peel and chop garlic. Clean and wash dill.

Heat oil in a *handi*/pan, add ginger and garlic, sauté over medium heat until light golden, add peppercorns and bay leaf, stir for a few seconds, add tomatoes, stir, cover and cook, stirring occasionally, until mashed. Then add 1 litre/4½ cups of water and dill, bring to a boil, reduce to low heat, cover and simmer, stirring occasionally, until reduced by three-fourths. Remove and force through a fine mesh soup strainer into a saucepan. Return gravy to heat, add *deghi mirch*, clove powder and salt, stir, reduce to low heat and simmer until of sauce consistency. Now add nutmeg, stir, remove, adjust the seasoning and keep warm.

COOKING

Heat oil in a *kadhai*/wok, dip the paneer "sandwiches" in the batter and deep-fry over medium heat until golden. Remove to absorbent paper to drain the excess fat.

TO SERVE

Make 4 beds of equal quantities of gravy on each of 4 individual plates, arrange a fried sandwich on each and serve as a starter.

Muttar ki Kachori

Yield: 12
Preparation Time 1:30 hours
Cooking Time 10 minutes/set

INGREDIENTS

The Dough
250g/2 cups	Flour
1g/¼ tsp	Soda bi-carb
	A pinch Salt
75ml/5 Tbs	Cooking Oil
	Desi Ghee/Clarified Butter to deep-fry

The Peas
350g/13 oz	Green Peas
45g/1½ oz	Desi Ghee/Clarified Butter
2g/1 tsp	Jeera/Cumin Seeds
	Salt
4	Green Chillies (seed & finely chop)
20g/2" piece	Ginger (finely chop)
	A generous pinch of Heeng/Asafoetida (reserve in 15ml/1 Tbs of water)
4.5g/1½ tsp	Dhania/Coriander Powder
3g/1 tsp	Yellow (or red) Chilli Powder
6g/2 tsp	Amchoor/Mango Powder
24	Raisins
15ml/1 Tbs	Lemon Juice

PREPARATION

THE DOUGH: Sift flour, soda bi-carb and salt together, make a bay, pour oil in it and start mixing gradually. When the oil is fully mixed, add water (approx 100ml/7 Tbs) and knead to make soft dough. Cover with moist cloth and keep aside for 15 minutes. Divide into 12 equal portions, make balls and cover with moist cloth. Flatten each ball between the palms into discs approx 3" diameter, ensuring it is thinner around the edges.

THE PEAS: Heat *ghee* in a *handi*/pan, add cumin, stir over medium heat until it begins to pop, add chillies and ginger, stir, add asafoetida and stir until the moisture evaporates (approx 10 seconds). Add coriander powder and yellow (or red) chilli powder (dissolved in 30ml/2 Tbs of water) and stir until the moisture evaporates. Then add the green peas, cook, stirring occasionally, sprinkling small quantities (not more than 10ml/2 tsp) at regular intervals, until *al dente* (almost cooked; approx 10-12 minutes). Now add salt and *amchoor*, stir. Remove, adjust the seasoning, add the raisins, stir to mix, sprinkle lemon juice, stir and divide into 12 equal portions.

THE STUFFING: Place a portion of the stuffing in the middle, enfold and pinch off the excess dough to seal the edges. Then flatten between the palms into discs (approx 2½" diameter).

COOKING

Heat *ghee* in a *kadhai* and deep-fry *Kachori* over medium heat until golden brown and crisp. Remove to absorbent paper to drain off the excess fat.

TO SERVE

Paper a paper doiley on a silver platter, arrange the *Kachori* on top and serve with *Saunth*/Ginger Powder.

Til ki Tikki Tamater ki Tari Marua Aloo ke Saath

Serves: 4

Preparation Time
1:30 hour

Cooking Time
45 minutes

INGREDIENTS

The Croquette

400g/14 oz	*Paneer*
250g/9 oz	*Bhein/Nadru*/Lotus Root
15ml/1 Tbs	Lemon Juice
110g/¼ lb	French Beans
125g/¼ lb	Carrots
30g/1 oz	Green Peppercorns
15g/1½" piece	Ginger
8	*Guchchi*/Morels
75g/2½ oz	Flour
1.75g/1½ tsp	*Marua*/Marjoram
3g/1 tsp	White Pepper Powder
	Salt
	Safaed Til/Sesame Seeds to sprinkle
	Cooking oil to deep-fry

The Eggplant & Potatoes

200g/7 oz	*Baingan*/Brinjals
	Cooking oil to shallow-fry eggplant
4	Potatoes (medium)
	Butter to grease roasting tin/tray
30g/1 oz	Onions
150g/5 oz	Yoghurt
150ml/5 oz	Cream
1.75g/12 tsp	*Marua*/Marjoram
2.25g/¾ tsp	White Pepper Powder
	Salt

PREPARATION

THE *PANEER*: Grate in a bowl.

THE LOTUS ROOTS: Peel, rinse thoroughly, grate, put in a *handi*/pan, add lemon juice and enough water, boil until tender. Drain, cool, squeeze in a napkin to ensure there is no moisture and then finely chop to obtain coarse mince.

THE REMAINING VEGETABLES: String beans, wash, finely chop, blanch in salted boiling water for 4-5 minutes, drain, refresh in iced water, drain and pat dry. Peel carrots, wash, finely chop, blanch in salted boiling water for 8-10 minutes, drain, refresh in iced water, drain and pat dry. Peel, wash and finely chop ginger.

THE PEPPERCORNS: Drain and pat dry.

THE MORELS: Soak in hot water for 10 minutes, drain, wash in running water to remove grit, soak again in hot water for 5 minutes. Drain and finely chop.

THE CROQUETTE: Put the lotus roots, vegetables, peppercorns and morels in the bowl with the paneer, add 30g/1 oz of flour, marjoram, pepper and salt, mix well, divide into 20 equal portions, make croquettes and refrigerate.

THE BATTER: Put the remaining flour in a bowl, add 90ml/6 Tbs of water and make a batter, ensuring there are no lumps.

THE EGGPLANT & POTATOES: Remove stems, wash, pat dry, cut eggplant vertically and then make half moon slices approximately ¼" thick by cutting horizontally. Sprinkle a little salt and keep aside to drain the moisture. Whisk yoghurt in a bowl, stir-in cream, season with marjoram, pepper and salt, keep aside.

Wash, peel and keep potatoes in a pan of cold water. Peel, wash and finely chop onions. Grease an 8" x 6" x 2" roasting tin with butter, sprinkle the onions evenly over the surface of the tin, cut potatoes into the thinnest possible slices (like potato wafers and pile the slices of each potato separately. Then arrange the piles two abreast and carefully spread the potatoes by pressing gently with the fingertips (taking care that the slices do not break and ensuring that they cover the tray as fully as possible to prevent the yoghurt and cream mixture from seeping through). Evenly spread the yoghurt and cheese mixture over the potatoes ensuring that they are not totally covered.

Heat the potatoes until the cream mixture comes to a boil and then transfer the tin to a pre-heated oven (350°F—top and bottom heat) and bake until potatoes are golden brown and the cream is of custard consistency. (The fat will leave the sides and the process will take 20-25 minutes.)

The Sauce

500g/1lb 2 oz	Tomatoes
120ml/½ cup	Cooking Oil
60g/2 oz	Onions
15g/½ oz	Garlic
25g/2½" piece	Ginger
30g/1 oz	Carrots
8	Black Peppercorns
2	*Tej Patta*/Bay Leaf
1.5g/½ tsp	White Pepper Powder
	Salt
7.5g/1¾ tsp	Red Chilli Paste
10g/1 tsp	*Beurre Manie*

The Garnish

300g/11 oz	Broccoli
50g/¼ cup	Butter

THE SAUCE: Remove eyes, wash and roughly chop tomatoes. Peel, wash and roughly chop onions and carrots. Peel garlic. Scrape, wash and roughly chop ginger.

Heat oil in a pot, add onions and garlic, sauté over medium heat until onions are translucent and glossy, add the carrots, ginger, peppercorns and bay leaves, stir for 5-6 minutes, add tomatoes, stir, cover and cook, stirring occasionally, until mashed. Then add 1 litre/4¼ cups of water, bring to a boil, reduce to low heat, cover and simmer, stirring occasionally, until reduced by three-quarters.

Remove and force through a soup strainer into a saucepan. Return sauce to heat, add white pepper and salt, stir, reduce to low heat, add chilli paste and *beurre manie*, stir and then simmer until of sauce consistency. Remove, adjust the seasoning and keep warm.

THE ACCOMPANIMENTS: Clean broccoli, trim the stems, blanch in salted boiling water for 2 minutes, drain, refresh in iced water, drain and pat dry.

COOKING

Heat oil in a *kadhai*/wok. Dip the croquettes in the batter, sprinkle sesame seeds scantily and deep-fry over medium heat until golden. Remove to absorbent paper to drain the excess fat. Keep warm.

To cook the eggplant, heat oil in a frying pan to smoking point, drain and add brinjal slices, shallow-fry over high heat until brown and crisp. Remove to absorbent paper to drain the excess fat. Keep warm.

To prepare the garnish, melt better in a frying pan, add the blanched broccoli and glaze over very low heat for one minute. Remove and keep warm.

TO SERVE

Place an equal quantity of eggplant slices in a star shape in the middle of each of 4 individual plates and pour an equal quantity of the sauce on top. Arrange an equal quantity of the potatoes on the sauce, place five croquettes evenly spaced in a circle at the periphery of the plate arranging the broccoli florets between them and serve hot.

Mirchiwala Paneer

Serves: 4

Preparation Time
25 minutes

Cooking Time
15 minutes

INGREDIENTS

24	*Paneer* (1" cubes)
	Sesame/Groundnut oil to deep-fry *paneer*
45ml/3 Tbs	Sesame/Groundnut Oil
6 flakes	Garlic
10g/1" piece	Ginger
110g/1 cup	Onions
2	*Harri Shimla Mirch*/Green Bell Peppers
2	Fresh Red Chillies
5ml/1 tsp	Soya Sauce
15ml/1 Tbs	Chilli Sauce
60ml/2 oz	Tomato Purée
3g/1 tsp	*Chakriphool*/Star Anise Powder
	Salt

The Batter

45g/1½ oz	*Arraroot*/Cornflour
45g/1½ oz	Flour
	Salt
1.5g/½ tsp	*Chakriphool*/Star Anise Powder
5ml/1 tsp	Sesame/Groundnut Oil

PREPARATION

THE VEGETABLES: Peel and finely chop garlic. Scrape, wash and finely chop ginger. Peel, wash and finely chop onions. Remove stems, wash, halve, seed and cut capsicum and red chillies into juliennes.

THE BATTER: Sift the two flours, add the remaining ingredients and 60ml/¼ cup of water, mix well. Reserve the *paneer* in the batter for 15 minutes.

COOKING

Heat oil in a *kadhai*/wok or a frying pan, add the *paneer* and deep-fry over medium heat until light golden (approx 2-3 minutes for each set). Remove to absorbent paper to drain excess fat. Transfer to a platter and keep warm. Reserve the oil.

To prepare the sauce, reheat 45ml/3 Tbs of the reserved oil in a *kadhai*/wok, add garlic, sauté over low heat until brown, add ginger and onions, stir for 15 seconds, add soya sauce and stir. Then add chilli sauce, stir, add tomato purée, star anise and salt, stir, add capsicum and red chillies, stir for a minute. Now add water, stir for a few seconds and remove. Adjust the seasoning.

TO SERVE

Arrange 6 cubes of *paneer* and equal quantities of the "masala" on each of 4 individual plates, spread tossed juliennes of carrots and beans on the side and serve as a starter.

Paneer Jaipuri

Serves: 4
Preparation Time 15 minutes
Cooking Time 45 minutes

INGREDIENTS

The Paneer

800g/1 lb 5 oz	Paneer
90g	Desi Ghee/Clarified Butter
3	Chhotti Elaichi/Green Cardamom
2	Lavang/Cloves
1 stick	Daalcheeni/Cinnamon (1")
90g/3 oz	Onions
20g/3½ tsp	Garlic Paste (strain)
10g/1¾ tsp	Ginger Paste (strain)
250g/1 cup	Yoghurt
60g	Fried Onion Paste
30g/1 oz	Cashew Nut Paste
6g/2tsp	Dhania/Coriander Powder
3g/1tsp	Haldee/Turmeric Powder
3g/1tsp	Yellow Chilli Powder
720ml/3 cups	Vegetable Stock (or water)
	Salt
1.5g/½ tsp	Chhotti Elaichi/Green Cardamom Powder
0.75g/¼ tsp	Javitri/Mace Powder
0.375g/⅛ tsp	Daalcheeni/Cinnamon Powder
30 ml/2 Tbs	Cream
0.5g/1 tsp	Zaafraan/Saffron
30ml/2 Tbs	Cream

PREPARATION

THE *PANEER*: Cut into ½" thick slices and then with a paisley-shaped (or any other) cutter obtain 12 paisley-shaped *paneer* pieces.

THE ONIONS: Peel, wash, roughly chop, transfer to a blender, add 90ml/6 Tbs of water and make a purée.

THE YOGHURT MIXTURE: Put yoghurt in a bowl, add fried onion paste, cashew nut paste, coriander, turmeric, yellow chilli powder and salt, whisk and keep aside.

THE SAFFRON: Crush saffron threads with a pestle, reserve in lukewarm milk and then make a paste.

COOKING

Heat *ghee* in a *handi*/pan, add green cardamom, cloves and cinnamon, stir over medium heat until the cardamom changes colour, add onion puree, *bhunno*/stir-fry until translucent, add garlic and ginger pastes, *bhunno*/stir-fry until the moisture evaporates. Remove *handi*/pan from heat, stir-in the yoghurt mixture, return *handi*/pan to heat and *bhunno*/stir-fry until the fat leaves the sides. Now add vegetable stock (or water) and bring to a boil. Remove and pass the gravy through fine muslin into a separate *handi*/pan. Return the gravy to heat, bring to a boil, add *paneer* and simmer, stirring occasionally but carefully, until the gravy is of thin sauce consistency. Sprinkle the cardamom, mace and cinnamon powders, stir carefully, stir-in cream and the saffron, remove and adjust the seasoning.

TO SERVE

Make a bed of equal portions of the gravy, arrange 3 *paneer* pieces on the sauce and serve with bread of your choice or steamed rice.

Pudina Paneer

Serves: 4

Preparation Time
45 minutes

Cooking Time
25 minutes

INGREDIENTS

600g/1lb 5 oz	*Paneer* (1" long; ½" thick diamonds)
17.5g/½ cup	*Taaza Pudhina*/Mint Leaves (whole)
75g/6 Tbs	*Desi Ghee*/Clarified Butter
3	*Chhotti Elaichi*/Green Cardamom
2	*Lavang*/Cloves
10g/1¾ tsp	Ginger Paste (strain)
10g/1¾ tsp	Green Chilli Paste
250g/1 cup	Yoghurt
3g/1 tsp	White Pepper Powder
	Salt
60g/2 oz	Cashewnut Paste
1.5g/½ tsp	*Chhotti Elaichi*/Green Cardamom Powder
0.75g/¼ tsp	*Jaiphal*/Nutmeg Powder
30ml/2 Tbs	Cream

PREPARATION

THE YOGHURT MIXTURE: Put yoghurt in a bowl, add pepper and salt, and whisk to obtain a homogenous mixture.

COOKING

Heat *ghee* in a *handi*/pan, add mint and deep-fry until crisp. Remove to absorbent paper to drain excess fat. Reheat *ghee*, add cardamom and cloves, and stir over medium heat until the cardamom begins to change colour. Add ginger and green chilli pastes (alongwith 120ml/½ cup of water) and stir over medium heat until the moisture evaporates. Remove *handi*/pan from heat, stir-in the yoghurt mixture, return *handi*/pan to heat and *bhunno*/stir-fry until the fat leaves the sides, add cashew paste, *bhunno*/stir-fry until the fat leaves the sides, add water (approx 720ml/3 cups), bring to a boil, reduce to low heat and simmer, stirring occasionally, for 2-3 minutes. Now add *paneer*, stir, crush and add mint leaves, bring to a boil, reduce to low heat and simmer, stirring occasionally, for 2 minutes. Sprinkle the cardamom and nutmeg powders, and stir-in cream. Remove and adjust the seasoning.

Keri ki Launjee

Serves: 4
Preparation Time: 35 minutes
Cooking Time: 20 minutes

INGREDIENTS

The Dumplings

900g/2 lb		Raw Mangoes
5g/1 tsp		*Dhania*/Coriander powder
225ml/1 cup		Mustard Oil
5g/1 tsp		Red Chilli powder
3g/⅔ tsp		*Methi*/Fenugreek seeds
3g/ 2 tsp		*Haldee*/Turmeric
10g/4 tsp		*Saunf*/Fennel seeds
		Salt
2g/½ tsp		*Kalonji*/Nigella seeds
250g/1¼ cup		*Gurh*/Jaggery

PREPARATION

THE MANGOES: Peel, cut lengthwise into quarters and remove the kernel.
THE JAGGERY: Pound with a pestle.

COOKING

Heat oil in a *kadhai* to a smoking point, reduce to medium heat, add fenugreek and sauté until it begins to change colour (approx 15 seconds). Add fennel, *kalonji*, coriander, red chillies, turmeric and salt, stir, add mangoes and stir for 5 minutes. Then add jaggery and water (approx 120ml/2 cup), bring to a boil, cover and simmer, stirring occasionally, for 7-8 minutes. Remove and cool.

TO SERVE

Remove to a dish and serve as an accompaniment.

Makki ka Halwa

Yield: 1.3 kg/3 lb

Preparation Time
30 minutes

Cooking Time
1 hour

INGREDIENTS

500g/1 lb 2 oz	Sweet Corn Kernels (preferably fresh)
250g/1¼ cup	*Desi Ghee*/Clarified Butter
480ml/2 cups	Milk
100g/3 oz	*Khoya* (grate)
60g/2 oz	Coconut (remove brown skin & grate)
500g/1 lb/2 oz	Sugar
60g/2 oz	Raisins
3g/1 tsp	*Chhotti Elaichi*/Green Cardamom Powder
1g/2 tsp	*Zaafraan*/Saffron
24	Pistachio (blanch, cool, remove skin & cut into slivers)

PREPARATION

THE SAFFRON: Crush with a pestle or with the back of a spoon, reserve in 30ml/2 Tbs of lukewarm milk and then grind into a paste at the time of cooking.

COOKING

Heat *ghee* in a *kadhai*/wok, add corn, *bhunno*/stir-fry over low heat until deep golden, add milk and *khoya*, and *bhunno*/stir-fry until the milk is completely absorbed. Then add coconut, *bhunno*/stir-fry for a minute, add sugar and *bhunno*/stir-fry until the *halwa* thickens and begins to come off the sides of the *kadhai*/wok. Remove, add raisins, cardamom and saffron, and stir to mix well.

TO SERVE

Remove to silver bowl, garnish with pistachio slivers and serve hot.

The Marwar Menu

Kandhey ki Subzi

Serves: 4

Preparation Time: 25 minutes

Cooking Time 25 minutes

INGREDIENTS

1 Kg/2¼ lb	Onions (button)
45ml/3 Tbs	Cooking Oil
2g/1 tsp	*Jeera*/Cumin Seeds
30g/5 tsp	Garlic Paste (strained)
15g/2½ tsp	Ginger Paste (strained)
2	Green Chillies
9g/1 Tbs	*Dhania*/Coriander Powder
3g/1 tsp	*Haldee*/Turmeric Powder
3g/1 tsp	Red Chilli Powder
450g/1 lb	Tomatoes
	A pinch *Kasoori Methi* (crush between the palms)

The Filling

4.5g/1½ tsp	*Amchoor*
3g/1 tsp	*Dhania*/Coriander Powder
2.25g/¾ tsp	*Jeera*/Cumin Powder
1.5g/½ tsp	Red Chilli Powder
1.5g/½ tsp	*Haldee*/Turmeric Powder
	Salt
	A pinch of Black Rock Salt

PREPARATION

THE ONIONS: Peel, wash and make criss-cross incisions on top for filling.

THE FILLING: Mix all the ingredients in a bowl.

THE STUFFING: Pack equal quantities of the filling between the incisions of the onions and reserve for 30 minutes.

THE GRAVY: Wash green chillies, slit, deseed, finely chop and discard the stems. Remove eyes, wash, quarter and chop tomatoes. Clean, wash and chop coriander.

COOKING

Heat oil in a *kadhai*, add cumin, stir over medium heat until it begins to crackle, add the garlic and ginger pastes, *bhunno*/stir-fry until the moisture evaporates, add green chillies and *bhunno*/stir-fry for a minute. Then add coriander, red chillies and turmeric (all dissolved in 45ml/3 Tbs of water), stir for a minute, add tomatoes and *bhunno*/stir-fry until the tomatoes are completely mashed. Now add the onions and salt, stir, reduce to low heat, cover and cook, stirring occasionally, until the onions are cooked, but not squishy and soft. Sprinkle kasoori methi, stir, remove and adjust the seasoning.

TO SERVE

Remove to serving dish, garnish with coriander and serve with *Chappati* or *Phulka*.

Papad Methi ki Subzi

Serves: 4
Preparation Time 30 minutes
Cooking Time 25 minutes

INGREDIENTS

12	Papad
500g/1lb 2 oz	*Taazi Methi*/Fenugreek
45ml/3 Tbs	Cooking Oil
2g/1 tsp	*Jeera*/Cumin Seeds
200g/7 oz	Onions
6 flakes	Garlic
7.5g/1¼ tsp	Ginger Paste (strain)
7.5g/1¼ tsp	Garlic Paste (strain)
2	Green Chillies
3g/1 tsp	*Dhania*/Coriander Powder
3g/1 tsp	*Haldee*/Turmeric Powder
2.25g/¾ tsp	Red Chilli Powder
200g/7 oz	Tomatoes
	Salt
15ml/1 Tbs	Lemon Juice

The Garnish

12.5g/1 Tbs	*Desi Ghee*/Clarified Butter
3.25g/1 Tbs	*Taaza Dhania*/Coriander
5g/½" piece	Ginger
5ml/1 tsp	Lemon Juice

PREPARATION

THE PAPAD: Roast until crisp and keep aside.
THE FENUGREEK: Clean, wash and finely chop.
THE VEGETABLES: Peel, wash and finely chop onions. Peel and finely chop garlic. Remove stems, wash, slit, seed and finely chop green chillies. Remove eyes, wash and chop tomatoes.
THE GARNISH: Clean, wash and chop coriander. Scrape ginger, wash, cut into juliennes and reserve in the lemon juice.

COOKING

Heat oil in a *handi*/pan, add cumin seeds, stir over medium heat until they begin to crackle, add onions and garlic, sauté until onions are light golden, add the ginger and garlic pastes, and *bhunno*/stir-fry until onions are golden. Then add green chillies and stir for a few seconds, add coriander, turmeric and red chilli powders (dissolved in 30ml/2 Tbs of water), and stir for a minute. Add tomatoes and *bhunno*/stir-fry until the tomatoes are completely mashed. Now add fenugreek and salt, *bhunno*/stir-fry until the fenugreek is cooked (approx 10 minutes), crush and add the *papad* and lemon juice, stir gently, remove and adjust the seasoning.

TO SERVE

Remove to a serving dish, pour on the *ghee*, garnish with coriander and ginger, serve with *Roti*.

Bhunnee Besan ki Masaledaar Bhindee

Serves: 4
Preparation Time
30 minutes
(plus time taken to pickle ginger)
Cooking Time
5 minutes

INGREDIENTS

800g/1¾ lb	*Bhindee*/Okra (small-size)
	Cooking Oil to deep-fry Okra
65ml/5 Tbs	*Desi Ghee*/Clarified Butter
60g/2 oz	*Besan*/Gramflour
9g	*Dhania*/Coriander Powder
6g	*Amchoor*/Mango Powder
3g/1 tsp	Red Chilli Powder
3g/1 tsp	*Haldee*/Turmeric Powder
	Salt
3g/1 tsp	Black Pepper Powder (freshly broiled & coarsely ground)
1.5g/½ tsp	*Motti Elaichi*/Black Cardamom Powder
0.75g/¼ tsp	*Jaiphal*/Nutmeg Powder

The Garnish

10g/1" piece	Ginger
15ml/1 Tbs	Lemon Juice
5ml/1 tsp	Sugar Syrup (thin)

PREPARATION

THE OKRA: Wash in running water, pat dry, slice off the caps and the tips and then make slits.

Heat enough oil in a *kadhai*/wok, add the okra and deep-fry until crisp. Remove to absorbent paper to drain the excess fat.

THE GARNISH: Scrape, wash and cut ginger into fine juliennes. Mix sugar syrup with lemon juice and reserve the juliennes in it for at least 2 hours.

COOKING

Heat *ghee* in a *kadhai*/wok, add gramflour, *bhunno*/stir-fry until it emits its unique aroma, add the fried okra, add coriander, *amchoor*, red chilli and turmeric powders (dissolved in 45ml/3 Tbs), stir, sprinkle salt, and stir until the gramflour coats the okra. Sprinkle pepper, cardamom and nutmeg powders, remove and adjust the seasoning.

TO SERVE

Remove to a service dish, garnish with pickled ginger and serve as a main course with *Poori* or *Phulka* or as an accompaniment.

Note: All weights are nett, i.e. post PREPARATION, and not gross.

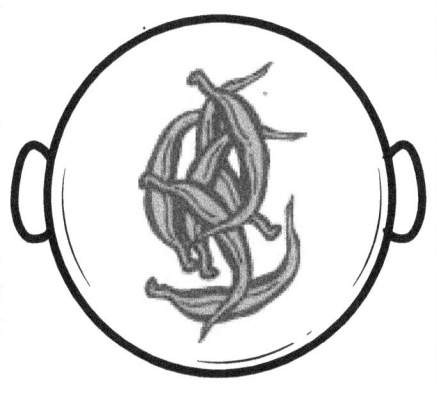

Chatpatti Gobhi

Serves: 4
Preparation Time 40 minutes
Cooking Time 20 minutes

INGREDIENTS

800g/1 lb 13 oz	Cauliflower (medium florets; reserve in salted iced water)
	Salt
45g/5 Tbs	Cooking Oil
2g/1 tsp	*Jeera*/Cumin Seeds
20g/2" piece	Ginger (finely chop)
8	Green Chillies (seed & finely chop)
250g/9 oz	Fresh Tomato Purée
6g/2 tsp	*Dhania*/Coriander Powder
3g/1 tsp	*Amchoor*/Mango Powder
1.5g/½ tsp	Red Chilli Powder
1.5g/½ tsp	Black Pepper Powder (freshly & coarsely ground)
	A generous pinch *Kasoori Methi*

The Potatoes

4	Potatoes (large)
3g/1 tsp	Red Chilli Powder
15g/½ oz	*Besan*/Gramflour
	Cooking oil to deep-fry
	Salt

PREPARATION

THE TOMATO PURÉE: Put in a bowl, add coriander, red chillies, *amchoor* and red chillies, stir to mix well.

THE POTATOES: Wash thoroughly but do not remove the skin, quarter and then halve each quarter lengthways. Sprinkle red chillies and salt, reserve for 15 minutes, sprinkle gramflour and mix well. Heat oil in a *kadhai*, add the potatoes and deep-fry over medium heat until cooked, golden and crisp.

COOKING

Heat oil in a *kadhai/wok*, add cumin seeds, stir over medium heat until they begin to pop, add ginger and green chillies, stir for 10 seconds, add the tomato purée mixture and stir for a few seconds. Then add cauliflower and salt, reduce to low heat, cover and cook until the cauliflower is almost cooked. Now add potatoes and stir until the moisture has completely evaporated. Sprinkle pepper and stir carefully. Crush *kasoori methi* between the palms, sprinkle, stir carefully, remove and adjust the seasoning.

TO SERVE

Remove to a service dish, garnish with pomegranate and serve with *Tandoori Paratha*, *Bidari Paratha* or *Poori*.

Dhania Aloo Mongodi

Serves: 4

Preparation Time
45 minutes

Cooking Time
10 minutes

INGREDIENTS

250g/9 oz	*Taaza Dhania*/Coriander (roughly chop)
4	Potatoes (medium; ½" cubes)
150g/5 oz	*Mongodi* (*Urad Daal*)
	Cooking Oil to deep-fry *Mongodi*
50g/¼ cup	*Desi Ghee*/Clarified Butter
4g/2 tsp	*Jeera*/Cumin Seeds
20g/2" piece	Ginger (finely chop)
240g/1 cup	Fresh Tomato Purée
9g/1 Tbs	*Dhania*/Coriander Powder
3g/1 tsp	Red Chilli Powder
3g/1 tsp	*Haldee*/Turmeric Powder
	Salt
2.25g/¾ tsp	Black Pepper Powder (freshly & coarsely ground)

PREPARATION

THE POTATOES: Boil in salted boiling water until *al dente* (which means nine-tenths cooked, not soft and squishy), drain and keep aside.

THE *MONGODI*: Heat oil in a *kadhai*/wok, add the *mongodi* and deep-fry until golden. Remove to absorbent paper to drain excess fat and then reserve in a panful of water until ready to cook.

THE TOMATO PURÉE: Put in a bowl, add coriander, red chillies and turmeric, stir to mix well.

COOKING

Heat *ghee* in a *kadhai*/wok, add cumin seeds, stir over medium heat until they begin to pop, add garlic and ginger pastes, and *bhunno*/stir-fry until the moisture evaporates. Add the fresh, chopped coriander, *bhunno*/stir-fry until the moisture evaporates add coriander, red chilli and turmeric powders (dissolved in 60ml/3 cup of water) and *bhunno*/stir-fry until the moisture evaporates. Then add tomato purée, *bhunno*/stir-fry until the fat leaves the sides, add potatoes, *mongodi* and salt, *bhunno*/stir-fry for 2-3 minutes or until the coriander nappes the potatoes and the *mongodi*. Sprinkle pepper, green cardamom, cinnamon, nutmeg and *kasoori methi* powders, stir, remove and adjust the seasoning.

TO SERVE

Remove to a service dish, garnish with coriander and tomato juliennes. Serve either as a main course with *Poori* or as an accompaniment.

Mongodi ki Subzi

Serves: 4
Preparation Time
10 minutes
(Plus time taken to prepare dumplings)
Cooking Time
1 hour

INGREDIENTS

The Dumplings
240g/1¼ cups *Moong dal* (washed)
5g/1 tsp Red Chilli powder
  Salt
  Ghee to shallow-fry

The Masala
60g/5 Tbs *Ghee*
2g/1 tsp *Dhania*/Coriander seeds
3g/1 tsp *Jeera*/Cumin Seeds
  Heeng/A pinch Asafoetida
20g/4 tsp Coriander powder
3g/2 tsp Red Chilli powder
3g/2 tsp *Haldee*/Turmeric
10g/2 tsp *Amchoor*/Mango powder
  Salt

The Garnish
15g/2 cup Coriander

PREPARATION

THE Dumplings: Pick, wash in running water and soak *daal* for *not* more than 30 minutes. Drain, put in a blender, add red chillies and salt, make a coarse paste. Make grape-sized dumplings with a spoon and place them on a tray evenly spaced out. Dry in the sun until hard (at least 2 days). *Mongodi* has a shelf life of 6 months in an airtight container. Yield : approx 250g/9 oz.

The coriander: Clean, wash and chop.

COOKING

Heat ghee in a *kadhai*, add the dumplings and shallow-fry over medium heat until golden brown. Remove the dumping and reserve the fat.

Reheat 60g/4 Tbs of the reserved ghee, add the coriander and cumin seeds, sauté over medium heat until they begin to crackle, add asafoetida and stir. Add coriander powder, red chillies, turmeric and mango powder—all dissolved in water (approx 120ml/ ½ cup)—and stir constantly until the liquid has almost evaporated. Then add water (approx 600ml/2½ cups) and bring to a boil. Now add the fried *Mongodi* and salt, bring to a boil, cover and simmer until soft and coated with the gravy. Adjust the seasoning.

TO SERVE

Remove to a dish, garnish with coriander and serve with *Poori* or *Phulka*.

Note: To make *Mongodi* with *Kadhi,* use 100g/3½ oz of dumplings—to be fried and added half-way through the cooking process of *Kadhi*. However, to make the Marwari *Kadhi* use 50g/⅓ cup of gramflour and black salt instead of table salt.

Heeng Jeerey ke Aloo

Serves: 4

Preparation Time
30 minutes

Cooking Time
3-4 minutes

INGREDIENTS

600g/1 lb 5 oz	Baby Potatoes
	Salt
75g/6 Tbs	*Desi Ghee*/Clarified Butter
	A generous pinch of *Heeng*/Asafoetida
5g/2½ tsp	*Jeera*/Cumin Seeds
7.5g/¾" piece	Ginger (chop)
2	Green Chillies (seed & chop)
9g/1 Tbs	*Anaardaana*/Pomegranate Powder
3g/1 tsp	Red Chilli Powder
1.5g/½ tsp	*Haldee*/Turmeric Powder

The Garnish

1	Tomato (quarter, remove pulp & dice)
5g/½" piece	Ginger (juliennes; reserve in 30ml/2 Tbs of lemon juice)
3.25g/1 Tbs	*Taaza Dhania*/Coriander (chop)

PREPARATION

THE POTATOES: Put in a pan, add salt, cover with enough water and boil until cooked but not mushy. Drain and keep aside.

COOKING

Heat *ghee* in a *handi*/pan, add asafoetida, stir over medium heat until it puffs up, add cumin seeds, and stir until they begin to pop. Then add the ginger and green chillies, stir for 30 seconds, add potatoes and *bhunno*/stir-fry for a minute. Now add *anaardaana*, red chillies and turmeric, and *bhunno*/stir-fry until masala turns dark brown and evenly coats the potatoes. Remove and adjust the seasoning.

TO SERVE

Remove to a serving dish, garnish with tomato dices, ginger juliennes and coriander, serve with *Poori*.

Methi Kishmish

Serves: 8
Preparation Time
45 minutes
(plus time taken to soak fenugreek)
Cooking Time
10 minutes

INGREDIENTS

200g/7 oz	*Methi*/Fenugreek Seeds
45g/1½ oz	*Kaer* (Raw Mango - reserve in water until soft)
480ml/2 cups	Milk
120g/½ cup	Cooking Oil
	A generous pinch of *Heeng*/Asafoetida
15g/5 tsp	*Dhania*/Coriander Powder
6g/2 tsp	Red Chilli Powder
6g/2 tsp	*Haldee*/Turmeric Powder
30g/1 oz	*Amchoor*/Mango Powder
100g/3 oz	*Kishmish*/Raisins
	Salt

PREPARATION

THE FENUGREEK SEEDS: Clean and soak overnight in milk (in the refrigerator). Then bring to a boil over medium heat, reduce to low heat and simmer, stirring occasionally, until the milk is fully absorbed. Remove and wash the boiled fenugreek in running cold water, drain and keep aside.

COOKING

Heat oil in a *kadhai*/wok, add asafoetida, stir until it puffs up, add coriander, red chilli and turmeric (dissolved in 60ml/¼ cup of water) and *bhunno*/stir-fry until the moisture evaporates. Then add fenugreek seeds and *kaer*, stir for 4-5 minutes, add raisins, *amchoor* and salt, and stir for 1-2 minutes. Remove and adjust the seasoning.

TO SERVE

Remove to a service dish, and serve as an accompaniment.

Mawa Muttar

Serves: 4

Preparation Time
15 minutes

Cooking Time
8-10 minutes

INGREDIENTS

800g/5 cups	Green Peas
200g/7 oz	*Khoya* (grate)
50g/¼ cup	*Desi Ghee*/Clarified Butter
2.5g/1 tsp	*Shahi Jeera*/Royal Cumin Seeds
20g/2" piece	Ginger (cut into fine juliennes)
4	Green Chillies (halve, seed and discard the stems)
	A pinch Asafoetida (reserve in 30ml/2 Tbs of water)
200 ml/7 oz	Fresh Tomato Purée
3g/1 tsp	Red Chilli Powder
3g/1 tsp	*Dhania*/Coriander Powder
1.5g/½ tsp	*Haldee*/Turmeric Powder
	Salt
1.5g/2 tsp	*Chhotti Elaichi*/Green Cardamom Powder
	A generous pinch of *Motti Elaichi*/Black Cardamom
	A generous pinch of *Daalcheeni*/Cinnamon (1")
3g/1 tsp	Black Pepper Powder (freshly & coarsely ground)

PREPARATION

THE TOMATO PURÉE: Put in a bowl, add red chillies, coriander and turmeric, stir to mix well.

COOKING

Heat *ghee* in a *handi*/pan, add royal cumin seeds, stir over medium heat for a few seconds, add ginger, chillies and asafoetida, stir until the moisture evaporates. Then add the tomato purée mixture, *bhunno*/stir-fry until the fat leaves the sides, add green peas and salt, *bhunno*/stir-fry for
3-4 minutes, add 120ml/½ cup of water, bring to a boil, reduce to low heat and simmer until al *dente*. Now add *khoya*, increase to medium heat and stir until incorporated. Remove and adjust the seasoning. Sprinkle green cardamom, black cardamom, cinnamon and pepper, stir, sprinkle lemon juice, stir, remove and adjust the seasoning.

TO SERVE

Remove to a bowl, garnish with *chandi ka varq* covered *khoya* marbles, and serve with *Poori*.

Kadhi Pakorhi

Serves: 4
Preparation Time 2:20 hours
Cooking Time 20-25 minutes

INGREDIENTS

The *Kadhi*
500g/2 cups	Yoghurt (1-day old)
60g/2 oz	Gramflour
3g/1 tsp	Red Chilli Powder
3g/1 tsp	*Haldee*/Turmeric Powder
	Salt

The *Pakorhi*
100g/½ cup	Moong Daal
	Salt
	Cooking Oil to deep-fry Pakorhi

The Tempering
50g/¼ cup	*Desi Ghee* (Clarified Butter)
4g/2 tsp	*Jeera*/Cumin Seeds
2.25g/½ tsp	*Rai*/Mustard Seeds
	A generous pinch *Heeng*/Asafoetida
8	Whole Dried Red Chillies

PREPARATION

THE KADHI: Whisk yoghurt in a bowl, add the remaining ingredients and whisk to mix well. Then add 1.2 litres/4 cups of water and whisk again. (To get a *Kadhi* of better consistency, forget about yoghurt. Instead, use 1.7 litres/6 cups of *chaas*/butter milk.)

THE PAKORHI: Soak the lentils in water for 2 hours, drain, transfer to a blender, add salt and approx 120ml/½ cup of water and pulverise into a fluffy batter (akin to whipped cream). Remove and keep aside.

Heat oil in a *kadhai*, mentally divide the batter into 24 equal portions, make dumplings and deep-fry over medium heat until golden. Remove to absorbent paper to drain the excess fat.

THE TEMPERING: Wipe red chillies clean with moist cloth.

COOKING

Put the yoghurt (or buttermilk) mixture in a *handi*/pan, bring to a boil, reduce to low heat, cover and simmer, stirring occasionally, until of thin sauce consistency. Then add the fried *pakorhi*, bring to a boil, reduce to low heat and simmer, stirring occasionally, for 4-5 minutes.

Meanwhile, to prepare the tempering, heat *ghee* in a frying pan, add the cumin seeds, mustard seeds, stir over medium heat until the seeds begin to crackle, add asafoetida and stir until the asafoetida puffs up, add the red chillies and stir until they change colour (bright red), remove and pour over the simmering *Kadhi*. Remove and adjust the seasoning.

TO SERVE

Remove to a bowl and serve with *Chappati*, *Phulka* or steamed rice.

Urad ki Daal

Serves: 4

Preparation Time
45 minutes

Cooking Time
30 minutes

INGREDIENTS

The Lentil

250g/1¼ cups	*Urad Daal* (washed)
3g/1 tsp	*Haldee*/Turmeric Powder
4	Yellow Chillies
10g/1" piece	Ginger
	Salt
200g/1 cup	*Desi Ghee*/Clarified Butter
120ml/½ cup	Milk
2 drops	*Kewra*

The Tempering

50g/¼ cup	*Desi Ghee*/Clarified Butter
	A generous pinch *Heeng*/Asafoetida
2	Onions (small)

The Garnish

3.25g/1 Tbs	*Taaza Dhania*/Coriander
4	Lemon Wedges

PREPARATION

THE LENTIL: Pick, wash in running water, drain, soak in water for 30 minutes and drain again. Wipe yellow chillies clean with moist cloth. Scrape and wash ginger (keep the piece whole).

THE TEMPERING: Reserve asafoetida in 30ml/2 Tbs of water. Peel, wash and slice onions.

THE GARNISH: Clean, wash and chop coriander.

COOKING

Put 1 litre/4¼ cups of water in a *handi*/pan, add turmeric, yellow chillies, ginger and salt, bring to a boil, add the drained lentils, bring to boil, reduce to low heat, cover and simmer, stirring occasionally, until the *daal* is three-fourths cooked (approx 15 minutes). Drain, discard the ginger and keep aside.

Heat *ghee* in a *handi*/pan, add milk and *kewra*, bring to a boil, add the drained lentil, stir, reduce to low heat, cover and cook on *dum* until the lentil is cooked but not squishy or mashed (approx 15 minutes).

To prepare the tempering, melt *ghee* in a frying pan, add onions and sauté over medium heat until golden, add the reserved asafoetida, stir for a few seconds, pour over the cooked lentil, stir, remove and adjust the seasoning.

TO SERVE

Remove *daal* to a service bowl, garnish with coriander and serve with lemon wedges, *Phulka*, *Tandoori Roti*, *Paratha* or as an accompaniment.

Besan ke Gatte

Serves: 4
Preparation Time 1:15 hours
Cooking Time 30 minutes

INGREDIENTS

The *Gatte* (Dumplings)
265g/2½ cups	*Besan*/Gramflour
5g/1 tsp	Baking Soda
	Salt
100g/3 oz	Khoya
15g/1½" piece	Ginger
3.25g/1 Tbs	*Taaza Dhania*/Coriander
60g/2 oz	Yoghurt
25g/2 Tbs	*Desi Ghee*/Clarified Butter

The Filling
300g/11 oz	*Paneer*
60g/2 oz	Cheese (Processed or Cheddar)
30g/1 oz	Khoya
2.5g/1 tsp	*Shahi Jeera*/Black Cumin
6 sprigs	Basil (fresh)
2	Green Chillies
24	Roasted Pistachios
36	Raisins

The Gravy
100g/½ cup	*Desi Ghee* (Clarified Butter)
5 sticks	*Lavang*/Cloves
2 sticks	*Daalcheeni*/Cinnamon (1")
2g/1 tsp	*Jeera*/Cumin Seeds
A generous pinch	*Heeng*/Asafoetida
110g/1 cup	Onions (optional)
150g/5 oz	Tomatoes
250g/1 cup	Yoghurt
9g/1 Tbs	*Dhania*/Coriander Powder
3g/1 tsp	Red Chilli Powder
3g/1 tsp	*Haldee*/Turmeric Powder
	Salt
720 ml/3 cups	Vegetable Stock
1.5g/½ tsp	Black Pepper Powder
1.5g/½ tsp	*Chhotti Elaichi*/Green Cardamom Powder
0.75g/¼ tsp	*Lavang*/Clove Powder
0.375g/⅛ tsp	*Daalcheeni*/Cinnamon Powder
0.375g/⅛ tsp	*Javitri*/Mace Powder
3.25g/1 Tbs	*Taaza Dhania*/Coriander

PREPARATION

THE GATTE: Sift besan, baking soda and salt into a *paraat*. Scrape, wash and finely chop ginger. Clean, wash and finely chop coriander. Whisk yoghurt, mix with the gramflour, add the remaining ingredients and 180ml/¾ cup of water, knead to make a hard but pliable dough and divide into 4 equal portions.

THE FILLING: Grate paneer, cheese and khoya, then mash with the base of the palm. Clean, wash and finely chop basil. Wash green chillies, slit, seed, finely chop and discard the stems. Mix these and the remaining ingredients in a bowl, divide into 4 equal portions and make 5" long "logs".

THE STUFFING: Flatten the gramflour balls with the hand or a rolling pan into a rectangular shape (6" x 2½"). Using the thumb, make a channel, along the length and in the middle of the rolled out dough, place a "log" of the filling in the channel and fold over to make a roll. Seal the ends. Boil water in a steamer and steam the rolls for 30 minutes. Remove and keep aside.

THE GRAVY: Peel, wash and slice onions. Remove eyes, wash and chop tomatoes. Put yoghurt in a bowl, add coriander powder, red chillies and salt, whisk to mix well. Clean, wash and finely chop coriander.

COOKING

Heat ghee in a *handi*/pan, add cloves, cinnamon and cumin seeds, stir over medium heat until the cumin begins to crackle, add asafoetida, stir until it puffs up, add onions, *bhunno*/stir-fry over until light golden, add tomatoes and *bhunno*/stir-fry until the fat leaves the sides. Remove *handi*/pan from heat, stir-in the yoghurt mixture, *bhunno*/stir-fry the fat leaves the sides, add the vegetable stock, bring to a boil, reduce to low heat, add the steamed *gatta*, cover and simmer, stirring occasionally, until the gravy is of thin sauce consistency. Remove the *gatta*, pass the gravy through a fine mesh soup strainer into a separate *handi*/pan, add the *gatta*, return the *handi*/pan to heat, sprinkle black pepper, green cardamom, clove, cinnamon and mace powders, bring to a boil, remove and adjust the seasoning.

TO SERVE

Remove to a bowl, garnish with coriander and serve with *Chappati* or *Phulka*.

Moong Daal Khilma

Serves: 4

Preparation Time
1 hour

Cooking Time
2 hours

INGREDIENTS
300g/1½ cups	*Harra Moong*/Green Moong (reserve in water for 30 minutes)
4	Green Chillies (slit & seed)
3.25g/1 Tbs	*Sua/Soya*/Dill

The *Potli/Bouquet Garni*
10g/1" piece	Ginger (roughly chop)
2	*Motti Elaichi*/Black Cardamom
2	*Lavang*/Cloves
6	Black Peppercorns

The Tempering
75g/6 Tbs	*Desi Ghee*/Clarified Butter
2g/1 tsp	*Jeera*/Cumin Seeds
	A generous pinch of *Heeng*/Asafoetida Powder
3g/1 tsp	Red Chilli Powder
1.5g/½ tsp	*Haldee*/Turmeric Powder
	Salt
1	Tomato (large; quarter, remove pulp and dice)
	A generous pinch of Black Pepper (freshly roasted & coarsely ground)
	A generous pinch of *Motti Elaichi*/Black Cardamom Powder
	A generous pinch of *Chhotti Elaichi*/Green Cardamom
	A pinch of *Lavang*/Clove Powder
30ml/2 Tbs	Lemon Juice

PREPARATION

THE *BOUQUET GARNI*: Put all the ingredients in a mortar and pound with a pestle to break the spices, fold in a piece of muslin along with ginger and secure with enough string for it to hang over the rim of the *handi*/pan.

COOKING

Put 720ml/3 cups of water in a *handi*/pan, add *daal*, green chillies and *potli*, bring to a boil, reduce to low heat, cover and simmer, until *daal* is almost cooked, ensuring that it is not mashed, just soft. Uncover, remove and discard the *bouquet garni*.

To prepare the tempering, melt *ghee* in a frying pan, add cumin, stir over medium heat until it begins to pop, add asafoetida and stir until it puffs up. Then add red chillies, turmeric and salt (dissolved in 45ml/3 Tbs of water) stir until the moisture evaporates.

Now add cooked *daal*, stir for 4 minutes, ensuring that the lentil does not get mashed, add tomatoes and stir for a minute, ensuring that the lentil does not get mashed. Add pepper, black cardamom, green cardamom and clove powders, stir, add lemon juice, stir, remove and adjust the seasoning.

TO SERVE

Remove to a bowl, garnish with dill and serve as an accompaniment.

Daal Baati Churma

Serves: 4
Preparation Time 1:45 hours
Cooking Time 35-40 minutes

INGREDIENTS

The Daal
60g/2 oz	Channa Daal
60g/2 oz	Masoor Daal
60g/2 oz	Toor Daal
60g/2 oz	Moong Daal (washed)
60g/2 oz	Urad Daal (washed)
20g/1½ Tbs	Desi Ghee (clarified butter)
3g/1½ tsp	Jeera/Cumin Seeds
6.5g/2 Tbs	Dhania/Coriander
50g/½ cup	Onions
10g/1¾ tsp	Ginger Paste (strained)
10g/1¾ tsp	Garlic Paste (strained)
4.5g/1½ tsp	Red Chilli Powder
1.5g/½ tsp	Haldee/Turmeric Powder
	Salt
6g/2 tsp	Dhania/Coriander Powder

The Tempering
20g/1½ Tbs	Desi Ghee (clarified butter)
	A generous pinch Heeng/Asafoetida
2g/1 tsp	Jeera/Cumin Seeds

The Baati
500g/3½ cups	Atta (wholewheat flour)
6g/1 tsp	Baking Powder
7.5g/1½ tsp	Salt
100g/½ cup	Desi Ghee (clarified butter)
	Desi Ghee to soak Baati

PREPARATION

THE *DAAL*: Pick, wash in running water, drain and soak all five *daal* in a panful of water for 30 minutes. Drain at the time of cooking. Peel, wash and slice onions. Clean, wash and chop coriander.

Note: The original dish calls for only *channa* and *urad daal*. We felt that a combination of five *daal* would add a touch of exotica. The total quantity, however, would remain the same.

THE TEMPERING: Dissolve asafoetida in 15ml/1 Tbs of water.
THE *BAATI*: Sift *atta*, baking powder and salt into a *paraat*/tray or onto the work surface, make a bay, add melted *desi ghee* and start mixing gradually with the tips of the fingers to attain a sandy texture. When fully mixed, add water (approx 120ml/½ cup) and knead to make a hard dough. Cover with moist cloth and reserve for 20 minutes. Then divide into 20 equal portions, make balls, cover with moist cloth and reserve for 10 minutes. Now flatten the balls slightly to make *pedha* (approx 2½" diameter). Dust a baking tray with flour, arrange the *pedha* in it, cover with moist cloth and reserve until ready to bake.
THE OVEN: Pre-heat to 200°F.
THE *CHURMA*: Sift *atta* into a *paraat*/tray or onto the work surface, make a bay, add 30g/1 oz of melted *desi ghee* and start mixing gradually. When fully incorporated, add milk, knead to make a smooth dough, make patties, cover with moist cloth and reserve.
  Heat *desi ghee* in a *kadhai*/wok and deep-fry the patties over low-medium heat until golden. Remove, cool and crush the patties in a blender into a coarse powder. Remove and keep aside. Reserve the *desi ghee*.
  Heat the remaining (15g/½ oz) *desi ghee* in a frying pan, add the blended powder and *bhunno*/stir-fry over medium heat until it emits its unique aroma. Remove, cool, add the remaining ingredients, mix well, sprinkle a little water on the mixture only to make the handling easier, make *laddoo*—balls—with moist hands, cover and keep aside.

The *Churma*

145g/1 cup	*Atta* (wholewheat flour)
45g/1½ oz	*Desi Ghee* (clarified butter)
20ml/4 tsp	Milk
	Desi Ghee to deep-fry
35g/2½ Tbs	Castor Sugar
6	Almonds
10g/⅓ oz	*Mishri* (candied sugar)
5g/1 Tbs	Coconut
2g/⅔ tsp	Green Cardamom Powder

COOKING

Uncover and put the baking tray in the pre-heated oven for 30-35 minutes.

Meanwhile, heat *desi ghee* in a *handi*/pan, add cumin seeds, stir over medium heat until they begin to crackle, add the sliced onions, sauté until light golden. Add the ginger and garlic pastes, sauté until onions are golden brown. Now add the coriander, red chilli and turmeric powders (dissolved in 30ml/2 Tbs of water), *bhunno*/stir-fry until the moisture evaporates, add 720ml/3 cups of water, stir, add the drained lentils and salt, stir, bring to a boil, reduce to low heat and simmer until cooked (approx 25-30 minutes).

To prepare the tempering, heat *desi ghee* in a frying pan, add cumin seeds and stir until they begin to crackle, add asafoetida, stir for a few seconds over medium heat. Remove, pour the tempering over the *daal*. Cover immediately. Remove and adjust the seasoning. Sprinkle coriander.

Remove the *baati* from the oven, press the top to crack open the crust and soak in the reserved *desi ghee* for 10-12 seconds. Remove and keep aside.

TO SERVE

Serve the *baati* with *daal* and *churma* as a complete meal.

Balushahi

Yield: 30
Preparation Time 20 minutes
Cooking Time 50 minutes

INGREDIENTS

500g/4 cups	Flour
2g/¼ tsp	Baking Powder
200g/1 tsp	Soda bi-carb
200g/1 cup	Desi Ghee/Clarified Butter
50g/2 oz	Yoghurt
	Desi Ghee/Clarified Butter to deep-fry
	Chandi-ka-varq (optional)
5g/1½ tsp	Pistachio (slivers)
5g/2 tsp	Melon seeds

The Chasni

2 Kg/10 cups	Sugar
50ml/10 tsp	Milk

PREPARATION

THE DOUGH: Sift flour, baking powder and soda bi-carb together in a *paraat*, add the melted *ghee* and yoghurt, start mixing gradually. When fully mixed, add water (approximately 10 ml/2 tsp) and knead to make a hard dough, cover and keep aside for 15 minutes. Divide into 30 equal portions, make balls, flatten slightly to make *pedha* (approximately 1¼" diameter). Press the middle with the thumb to make a hole.

THE *CHASNI*: Put sugar in a *kadhai*, add water (approximately 2 litres/8½ cups) and milk, bring to a boil over high heat. Remove the scum and boil for another 20 minutes. Keep warm.
YIELD: 2 litres.

COOKING

Heat ghee in a *kadhai* and deep-fry the *pedha* over medium heat for five minutes. Reduce to very low heat and continue to fry for about 25 minutes. Then increase to medium heat and fry until golden brown (approximately 10 minutes). Remove and cool.

ASSEMBLING

Immerse the fried *Balushahi* in the *chasni* for about 10 minutes. Remove, sprinkle pistachio and melon seeds.

TO SERVE

Arrange on a silver platter or decorate with *varq* and serve.

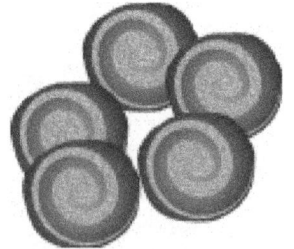

Kalakand

Yield: 1 kg

Preparation Time
10 minutes

Cooking Time
5 minutes

INGREDIENTS

1kg/2¼ lb	Danedar Khoya
200g/1 cup	Sugar
10kg/3 tsp	Pistachio (slivers)
	Chandi-ka-varq (optional)
	Desi Ghee to grease tray

PREPARATION
THE TRAY (12" x 6"): Grease with *ghee*.

COOKING
Heat *khoya* in a *kadhai*/wok, bring to boil over medium heat, stirring constantly with a flat spoon (*khurcha*) for five minutes. Remove, add sugar and stir until dissolved. Transfer the mixture immediately to the greased tray and level with a spatula, sprinkle pistachio and thump the tray on a table or on the floor to remove any air pockets. Keep aside to set.

TO SERVE
With the tip of a knife and a scale to guide, cut the set *kalakand* into 1¼" squares or any shape of your choice. Remove carefully (with a flexible spatula) to a silver platter. Cover with *varq* and serve.

Badaam Burfi

Yield: 36 pieces
Preparation Time 90 minutes

INGREDIENTS

1 kg/2¼ lb	Almonds
1g/2 tsp	*Zaafraan*/Saffron
60ml/¼ cup	*Gulaabjal* (Rose Water)
1 kg/5 cups	Sugar
25g/1 oz	Pistachio
	Chandi-ka-varq (silver leaves)

PREPARATION

THE ALMONDS: Soak overnight in a *handi*/pan, drain, add water and boil for five minutes. Remove a few almonds at a time from the boiling water, peel and grate. Spread the grated almonds on a table to dry. Then dry them in a double boiler. It is important to dry them by indirect heat to ensure that the almonds do not get coloured.

THE SAFFRON MIXTURE: Crush saffron with a pestle, soak in *gulabjal* for 10 minutes and then make a paste. (Use the small mortar-pestle, the sort used by vaid and hakim, which is also easily available in the market). Reserve one-fourth for garnish.

THE SYRUP: Boil sugar with water (approximately 1 litre/4¼ cups) in a *handi*/pan, skim and scum completely, reduce to low heat and simmer until of one-string consistence. Then add the saffron mixture and simmer until of slightly thicker than two-string consistency. Ensure that it does not achieve soft-crack or else the burfi will not set.

THE PISTACHIO: Blanch, cool, peel and cut into slivers.

ASSEMBLING

Put the dried, grated almonds in the hot syrup and mix well. Spread out the mixture on a clean, inverted metal tray and shape it into a square or a rectangle of 1" thickness. Then gently press the *burfi* with a moistened palm at regular intervals to remove the excess almond oil and syrup, using a kitchen towel to soak up the oozing liquid. (Cleanliness of the tray is of utmost importance to give the burfi a shelf life). Once the oil and syrup stops oozing, keep aside to set in a cool place.

TO SERVE

With the tip of a knife, cut the set burfi into 1½" squares or diamonds. Remove carefully with a flexible spatula to a silver platter, cover with *varq*, garnish with pistachio, sprinkle the remaining saffron mixture and serve.

Index

Aam ka Phajitha	K 34
Achaari Andey	3
Adlah	26
Akhaa Aad Dhungaar	18
Akhaa Peenda	19
Aloo ki Tehree	39
Amrud ki Subzi	33
Ande ka Halwa	K 35
Arbi ke Kebab	37
Badaam Burfi	78
Baingan Bemisaal	40
Baingan ki Launj	42
Balushahi	76
Besan ke Gatte	72
Bharri Harri Mirch ka Khaata	31
Bharwaan Parwal	43
Bharwaan Pasandey	28
Bhunnee Besan ki Masaledaar Bhindee	63
Bhunney Bharree Badhi Mirch	44
Bhunney Murg ke Pasandey	12
Bina Ghee ka Keema	K 14
Chaamp Badaami	29
Chakri Batia	K 32
Chandrakaar Paneer	49
Chatpatti Gobhi	64
Chimti Batiya	K 31
Daal Baati Churma	74
Dhania Aloo Mongodi	65
Dhania Khumb Mongodi	45
Ghuntwa Daal	K 25
Gobhi Rajwadi	30
Gol Maas Kaacher	23
Gunja	K 37
Handiwale Murg ke Pasandey	13
Hare Chane ka Halwa	K 36
Hare Chane ka Saag	K 19
Heeng Jeerey ke Aloo	67
Jaipuri Subz Seekh	38
Jholdar Andaa	K 28
Jowar ka Khichda	K 22
Kaalaa Murgh	K 12
Kadhi Pakorhi	70
Kakadi Jholdar Maans	K 13
Kalakand	77
Kandhey ki Subzi	61
Kebab Dashrath Singh	K 16
Keri ki Aanch	K 33
Keri ki Launjee	56
Khad	7
Khad Murg	6
Khadhe Masaley ka Gosht	14
Khadhe Masaley ka Murg	15
Kishmish ka Raita	K 29
Kitti	K 23
Laal Maas	20
Laddoo	K 38
Maalgoba	21
Maas ke Sooley	22
Maas ki Kadhi	17
Maaweywale Aloo	46
Machchi Jholdar	K 9
Makki ka Halwa	57
Makki ka Saag	K 18
Makki ka Soweta	27
Makki ki Khichdi	K 21
Malaai Kofta	47
Malai Kofta	K 20
Marua Aloo ke Saath	51
Mawa Muttar	35
Methi Dahi Machchi	K 10
Methi Kishmish	68
Mewar ka Khaas Maas	25
Mirchiwala Paneer	53
Mongodi ki Subzi	37
Moong Daal Khilma	73
Moong Daal Mogar	K 24
Murg ke Mokul	9
Murg ke Sooley	10
Murg ki Chaamp	16
Murg Sheora-Natwara	8
Murgh Korma	K 11
Muttar ki Kachori	50

Paneer Jaipuri	54	Sookhi Daal	K 26
Paneer ke Sooley	32	Soola	K 15
Papad Methi ki Subzi	62	Steamed Masala Andaa	K 27
Pudina Paneer	55	Tamatar ka Saag	K 17
Pyaaz ka Raita	K 30	Til ki Tikki Tamater ki Tari	51
Rasgulley ki Subzi	48	Urad ki Daal	71
Safaed Maas	24	Weights & Measures	xii
Scoop Lady Di	34		
Shorbedaar Murg	11		

www.ingramcontent.com/pod-product-compliance
Lightning Source LLC
Chambersburg PA
CBHW081133170426
43197CB00017B/2842